Celebrate!

Celebrate!

*Creative ideas and recipes for parties
with family and friends*

Contents

Introduction

A party can be held as a celebration of something, or just for fun – and since most parties are given at weekends or in the evenings, you could say they often simply celebrate not being at work, but having a chance to relax instead. Festive occasions celebrating some outstanding historical or religious event often turn into excellent parties. Parties are also given to celebrate sporting triumphs, or the award to someone of a special honor. Or you can just "party", as the youth culture of the turn of the millennium has it – go out dancing and enjoy the company of your friends. The whole idea of a party is to have a good time with people you like, in a pleasant, cheerful atmosphere.

If a party is to have a special character of its own, it needs to be well planned and prepared in advance. You must find the right setting, a place where your guests will feel comfortable and know that they are guaranteed a unique, one-off experience, remote from ordinary daily routine. We are not talking about huge events on a grand scale – the idea of this book is to show how even if financial means are limited, anyone can entertain friends without spending the earth. After all, something interesting happens almost every day, so any day can be a party, and a party is an excellent way to bring people together. It can even be a good breakfast party – something more leisurely than just quickly stoking up with food before the working day begins. A pretty table setting often creates a party atmosphere in itself.

The food is undoubtedly one of the most important elements in a party. Even for a small-scale occasion, the host should take the trouble to serve something special. Eating together encourages good conversation, either casual and relaxing or stimulating and full of surprises, while the guests are also enjoying delicious dishes. People who are not fond of cooking themselves can always order food sent in from their favorite restaurant, or if the restaurant itself is suitable they can hold the party there. Then there are large-scale occasions such as weddings when a party may go on for several days, giving both of the families and their friends a chance to get to know each other in a relaxed setting. Ideally, a party of that nature will be an experience remembered for decades to come, not just by the newly married couple but by the other guests as well.

Whatever the occasion for a party, both hosts and guests should have a good time. If you are always anxiously wondering whether everything is all right, you will pass your sense of anxiety on to your guests. Even if not so much as a drop of gravy has been spilt, the atmosphere will be spoiled. Hosts should be relaxed, offering their guests a friendly welcome and serving them with the very best their kitchens and cellars can provide. The best parties are given by people who strike just the right note for themselves and their friends. The ideas in this book are only suggestions to start your imagination working, and help you to throw parties which are very much your own.

Some comments

Beef Make sure you buy only top quality beef from a butcher you trust.
Ask where the beef you are buying was raised and where it was slaughtered.

Eggs Eggs used in the recipes in this book are medium unless otherwise stated.

Milk Milk used in these recipes is full-cream (whole milk) (3.5% fat content) unless otherwise stated.

Poultry Chicken and other poultry should always be cooked right through. Pricking the bird with a fork during cooking will show when it is done: if the juice which comes out is red or pink, you should cook it a little longer. Once the juice runs clear, the bird is ready.

Nuts Some of the recipes in this book contain nuts or nut oil. People who are allergic to nuts, or even inclined to be allergic, should not eat these dishes.

Herbs Use fresh herbs unless otherwise specified. If they are not available, they can be replaced by half the quantity of dried herbs.

The temperatures and cooking times given in the recipes refer to ordinary ovens. If you use a fan oven, adjust the directions according to the maker's instructions.
Total times given include both the preparation and the cooking time.

What kind of Party for what occasion?

There are as many kinds of parties as there are occasions for them. If you are not too sure of your talents for giving a party yet, start with something simple. An afternoon tea party, for instance, is an elegant way of asking people in to relax or just enjoy amusing conversation. A long, lazy brunch party is very welcome on Sundays and public holidays. Dinner parties or large evening parties, when the host wants to invite and entertain a considerable number of guests, call for rather more elaborate preparations.

All kinds of parties

CHAMPAGNE BREAKFAST A champagne breakfast is often just part of a large-scale festive occasion. Such events as weddings, or a family birthday party moving from one home to another, can last a whole day or even several days. But no matter how small the reason for it, a champagne breakfast is the ideal way to bring friends, relations or business colleagues together for relaxation and easy conversation. A champagne breakfast begins about ten or at the latest eleven in the morning, and should be over by about two in the afternoon. Mineral water and fruit juice should of course be available as well as champagne or other sparkling wines. If you decide to serve piquant little canapés, take into account the considerable time it takes to prepare them when planning your party. For a champagne breakfast lasting about an hour, eight canapés per guest is a good rule of thumb.

BRUNCH "Brunch", as the word suggests, is a cross between breakfast and lunch, and although an invitation to a long, leisurely breakfast of this kind may seem uncomplicated, it takes a good deal of preparation. The dishes you serve should be particularly good of their kind. There should be spare china available, since plenty of plates and dishes will be needed for the various kinds of food. China and cutlery (flatware) are not laid in table settings as usual but stacked on the sideboard. Guests can help themselves and sit down in informal groups, and the host does not have to work out a complicated seating plan for them. A successful brunch is the ideal way to start a relaxed Sunday, and in fact is suitable for almost any festive occasion. If the host has enough space to set a room aside as a children's playroom, brunch is a very good way to give their parents a pleasant break.

AFTERNOON TEA An afternoon tea party is a relatively inexpensive but stylish way of entertaining. It can be the prelude to an evening party on a larger scale, or lead up to a formal dinner by way of long drinks after tea. But a tea party can equally well just bring good friends or business acquaintances together for a couple of hours in the late afternoon, between four-thirty and six-thirty. You should serve carefully brewed tea with a selection of dainty sandwiches, biscuits (cookies), plain cake, and richer creamy cakes. Afternoon tea is thought of as very English, and another extremely British meal is high tea, when bread and butter and a selection of jams are served, as well as hearty meat or fish sandwiches, sauces, salads, and fresh vegetables.

DINNER A dinner party is the classic way of entertaining your friends. If you are planning a dinner at home, you will find preparation easier if you observe the following rules:
- If you are cooking for more than eight people, but have only the capacity of a normal household

kitchen, you risk being unable to spend enough time with your guests yourself.
- Never include a dish in the menu which you have not already tried out successfully.
- It is better to cook a simple dish leaving you time to talk to your guests, even while you are preparing the meal, than some ambitious haute cuisine creation which obliges you to hover over the stove, giving it your constant attention.
- The dishes should not have to be eaten the moment they are ready – choose recipes which will still be appetizing even if they have had to wait a little while, perhaps because some of the guests were late arriving, or the pre-dinner conversation has gone on rather a long time.
- If you are not quite sure of your guests' tastes, it is safer to avoid exotic ingredients and way-out recipes.
- Anything that can be made a few days before the dinner party should be prepared well in advance.

Dinner parties are usually given for personal friends, but in professional and business life in the United States it has always been correct etiquette to invite business acquaintances or the boss to dinner in your own home. Since the atmosphere is not quite as relaxed as among your friends and family, and the occasion may be to celebrate a successful business deal or may involve questions of promotion, a business dinner in a private house calls for perfect cooking, scrupulous etiquette, and stylish presentation.

EVENING PARTIES Relaxed informality is the keynote of the evening party. Guests do not come and go at any particular time; some may stay on until the early morning, while others leave after an hour to move on to another party. People help themselves to food and drink. The host's main responsibility at a party like this is to ask guests of different kinds with different backgrounds, so that interesting conversations can start up, and never to let the supply of drinks and canapés run out. The larger your home and the more varied the setting it provides, the more easily small groups can form, separate again after a while, and find other people to talk to. But even a one-roomed apartment can be the scene of a very successful party.

A THEMED PARTY Themed parties can be given at any time, not just on such occasions as Halloween. The theme can be inspired by your vacation – a Greek retsina party, a Californian barbecue – or can specify some special feature, for instance a "silk and velvet" party. Or you could keep up with modern trends and throw a Pokémon party. A "bad taste party" could even help you to clear out your wardrobe. The more ingeniously the theme is expressed in the food and drink, the decoration of your rooms and the clothes worn by your guests, the more fun the evening will be for everyone.

The right time

We might as well say at once that there is no absolutely right time to give a party; one of the guests you want to invite is bound to be unavailable. In practice, Fridays and Saturdays usually turn

out best for parties for friends and family, and Thursdays are often good for meetings with business acquaintances and professional colleagues. Unless you are giving a Christmas party, December is not a particularly good month. Parties tend to accumulate around the end of the year anyway, and people with busy social calendars often do not want any more invitations until the middle of January. On the continent of Europe, however, carnival time around March is a good party-giving season. The disadvantage of summer parties is that a number of potential guests may be away on vacation. So March to June and September to November are good times to throw a party – all you have to take into account is the possibility that it may clash with big outside events, particularly sporting fixtures (events). But with a little skill, good use of the space you have available, and a TV set, even a gripping Formula One race or a major football game can be included in your party, adding to the fun with its unpredictable and often exciting result.

The guest list

What guests you ask, and how many of them, will of course depend on the space that is available, how much money you want to spend, and the kind of party to which you are asking them. The smaller the party, the more important is the make-up of the guest list, and the greater the demands on the host's skill in persuading people to mix. Will your guests have anything to say to each other? Who tends to monopolize a conversation, and who prefers to listen? Who needs encouragement in order to join in a conversation at all? Drawing up a guest list for a party which is professionally important, rather than just for personal friends, can be very difficult for a host who is planning whom to invite and how to seat the guests.

If the party is held to celebrate an anniversary in your firm, then of course you must invite professional colleagues, but you need not necessarily invite their families. However, if you do, it can be very interesting and a plus for all concerned to bring people from different walks of life together. But it can sometimes be easier to do justice to different "target groups" by giving two smaller parties instead of one large one. The same is true of a children's birthday party, when the child's friends can come in for fun and games in the afternoon, and you can invite the grandparents and other family members in the evening.

These days, when divorce and separation are common, a host who is still on friendly terms with both former partners can face problems in drawing up a guest list. There is no general rule in such situations, and each case has to be decided on its merits: do the former partners still get on well? Or is animosity so deep that it could endanger the success of the whole party?

A delicate point when you are inviting people to a party concerns those pets, usually dogs, who often accompany their owners to social events. Whether the host invites this extra guest or not should depend on the character of the dog, who must not be likely to feel nervous in a large company of people. And you also have to bear the other guests in mind. If you are not sure whether they like dogs or not, it is best to ask people to leave their pets at home.

The invitation

The form of the invitation depends on the nature of the party. An invitation given orally or over the phone is not really a good idea unless the party is extremely informal. If it is, of course you can also

invite your guests by fax or e-mail, although it is sensible to follow up such an invitation with a phone call a few days before the party, unless the acceptance has already been confirmed.

But electronic communications themselves seem to have led to something of a revival of the invitation card, which is the perfect kind of invitation. It can vary from a simple printed card of the kind that can be bought in any stationer's, to a work of art lavishly designed on the computer by yourself, to illustrate the occasion for the party and let your prospective guests know they can expect something really special. The ideal invitation card consists of three parts:
• The text of the invitation itself, telling the recipient who is giving the party, where, when, and for what occasion.
• A reply section to be returned by the invited guests, accepting or refusing the invitation.
• A memo to be kept by the guests, repeating the facts of the invitation, and if necessary giving directions how to get to the party.

An invitation should not be issued too long before the party, and certainly not too close to it. In practice, the following timings have proved useful as guidelines:
• Eight weeks ahead for weddings or large birthday parties involving more than one household.
• Six weeks ahead for large parties and gatherings of a purely social nature.
• Four weeks ahead for dinners, buffets, small-scale parties and receptions.

The right Place
for a party

Not the least important factor in making your guests feel at ease and creating the right atmosphere is the place where you hold a party. If it is to be in your own home, you will want the guests to feel comfortable wherever they go in your house or apartment. Of course it is always possible to hire somewhere for a party: a restaurant, conference rooms in a hotel, or, for really large events, a town or village hall. And if you are looking for somewhere out of the ordinary, such places can also be found quite easily: a big barn on a farm, a historic railway train – there's no limit to the ingenious party-giver's imagination.

Outside the home

If you are throwing a party in a restaurant or hotel you will not usually have to worry about the logistics – it will simply depend on your budget, and the nature of the party, whether it is held in the back room of a village inn or the banqueting room of a grand five-star hotel. Other possibilities such as community halls, church halls or private theaters are not always suitable, since they may not be furnished with parties in mind, and the facilities may not be ideal. When you are thinking about hiring a place, therefore, you should ask yourself the following questions:

- How many people will it hold?
- How easily can the guests reach it? Can they get there by public transport? Is there a car park (parking lot) nearby? Will a shuttle service be needed?
- What facilities are available? Is there running water? Are the electrical installations in good order? Are there enough sockets? Are the safety

precautions satisfactory? If the answer to any of these is "no", then how does the place get its supplies of electricity and water?
- Are there toilets (rest rooms)? If not, where can you hire mobile ones?
- How can the hall or other location be divided up (into cloakroom, bar, buffet, live music, dancing)?
- Can food be cooked on the premises? Are there cooking facilities and the necessary china and cutlery (flatware)?
- How can food be kept hot during the party?
- Are there enough facilities for chilling drinks and cold dishes?
- Are there neighbors who might complain of the noise or of parked cars?
- What time limits are there on your use of the venue? When can you as host begin preparations? Will you have to bear in mind regulations about noise after a certain time of night? When, at the latest, will you have to vacate the premises? Will you have to clear up directly after the party or can you leave this until the day after?

BATHROOMS AND TOILETS If you are inviting friends to a home with one or more guest bathrooms, you must observe good hygiene, and make sure you have enough paper, soap, and hand towels. If guests will have to use the family bathroom, you should take a good look around that too; is everything spotlessly clean? Is the lock on the door in working order, and is there a key in it? Everything personal should be cleared away, and you could put some room perfume on a light bulb to get rid of unwanted odors.

THE LIVING ROOM The central scene of the party, the place where the guests assemble, should of course be very carefully inspected. In small parties of people who know each other well, conditions can be a little more cramped than is ideal, but otherwise, as a rule of thumb, there should be about one and a half square metres (yards) of space for every guest. With this in mind, ask yourself the following questions:

- How big is the room?
- Will furniture have to be moved out or pushed against the walls?
- Are there any delicate or particularly valuable pieces of furniture which must be protected from possible damage?
- Where will your guests be eating?
- Is there enough seating in the room?
- Are there enough surfaces where people can put down plates and glasses?
- Will part of the room have to be kept free as a dance floor or stage?
- Can the balcony, patio, garden or garage be used to extend the space where you are planning to hold the party?

Sometimes a diagram of the room to scale will give you a useful overall view, making it possible to work out on paper various ways of using the available space before you send out invitations.

In your own home

ON ARRIVAL: THE HALL, THE CLOAKROOM

Many entrance halls in apartments or private houses are on rather a small scale even for the family's daily use. When you have invited guests, the first thing to do is move your own clothes out of the cloakroom, to leave space for the coats of the guests you are expecting. If there is no cloakroom or hanging space, it is usually a good idea to turn a bedroom into a temporary cloakroom – it will not be in use during the party anyway. If there is to be dancing, or if the streets are full of slushy snow, people may want to change their shoes when they arrive. Another point is to remember to provide a place where wet umbrellas can dry off in rainy weather.

The Kitchen
the heart of the party

All the delicacies which the guests will enjoy eating later are made in the kitchen. You could call it the engine-room of the party, and you need good, functional kitchen equipment. But if your kitchen is well equipped for ordinary everyday use, preparations for a party will hold no terrors. However, the large number of different dishes may place something of a strain on the quantity of kitchen utensils you use, the number of hobs or gas rings (burners) available, and the storage space you will need, if only for a short period of time.

Equipment

POTS AND PANS How much work you have to do in the kitchen of course depends first and foremost on what food you are planning to serve your guests. Only the minimum basic equipment is necessary for making the canapés to serve at a champagne breakfast. But if you are planning more of a full gourmet meal, it is a good idea to borrow extra pots and pans from friends and neighbors, and if necessary some extra portable hobs or gas rings (stoves or burners), just for the duration of the party. Soufflé dishes are very versatile and usually decorative too, and can also be bought as individual ramekins. Shallow white ovenproof china dishes are suitable for pizzas and quiches.

KITCHEN UTENSILS It is a good idea to make life as easy for yourself as possible and begin preparations in the kitchen in good time. If you have a freezer, cook suitable dishes in advance and freeze them. Goulash, sliced meat in a sauce, fricassees, ragouts, large roast joints, roulades, one-pot dishes, soups, broths and casseroles can all easily be made a few days ahead of the party and frozen. However, you should remember that home-made dishes, unlike commercial frozen convenience foods, should not be kept longer than three months. Deep-frozen bread rolls will be nice and crisp after a few minutes in the oven, and will taste freshly baked. However, flash-fried or grilled (broiled) meat, most fish dishes and salads must be served freshly prepared. Food preparation machines with the widest range of attachments possible to perform various different functions are very useful too, whether they stand on the kitchen counter or are hand-held. They will help you to make cream soups, sauces, relishes, dips and desserts easily. A deep-fryer is ideal for chips (French fries). Hotplates or hostess trolleys are

Basic kitchen equipment

- Baking sheet
- Can opener
- Cherry and olive stoner (pitter)
- Chopping board
- Egg slicer
- Fish slice (spatula)
- Forcing bag (with various attachments)
- Frying pans (skillets) (various sizes, with and without non-stick linings)
- Garlic press
- Grater
- Ice crusher
- Kitchen scales (measuring cups)
- Kitchen scissors
- Kitchen tongs
- Kitchen towels
- Knives (bread knife, carving knife, chopping knife, kitchen knife, knife to make decorative shapes, mezzaluna, paring knife, serrated knife, vegetable knife)
- Lemon squeezer (juicer)
- Measuring jug
- Mincer (grinder)
- Mixing bowls (stainless steel, various sizes)
- Non-stick baking paper
- Nutcrackers
- Pastry brush
- Pastry cutters
- Pastry wheel
- Peppermill
- Pestle and mortar
- Plastic containers (various sizes)
- Saucepans (stainless steel, various sizes)
- Sieve (strainer)
- Skimmer
- Spring-clip baking tin (spring form pan)
- Truffle scraper
- Whisk
- Wooden spoons

useful for keeping hot foods at the right temperature during the party. With the aid of such devices even the host can enjoy a relaxed, entertaining evening without having to keep rushing off to the kitchen all the time.

PARTY CATERING Among the services now more widely available is party catering. Catering firms take most of their orders from organizers of business receptions and office parties, but private party-givers can use a caterer to spare them some or all of the work of food preparation. The range of services on offer is very varied, and so are the prices charged: butchers, delicatessen stores, restaurants and hotels will now often offer their services outside their own premises. Other firms specialize in catering for big occasions, and besides preparing and delivering food and drink, will also provide all the necessary equipment, from coffee spoons to a marquee accommodating a thousand people. If you are thinking of calling on professional help for all or some of the preparations for a party, take a little time to look at the different services on offer, comparing prices and above all quality. After all, your reputation as a host is at stake.

Foodstuffs

STAPLE INGREDIENTS There are said to be some culinary artists who can put together a delicious menu at any time from whatever leftovers they find in the fridge. But most of us are not among them, so it is wise to make sure that you always have a good supply of staple foodstuffs ready to hand. What exactly they are will of course depend on your personal preferences.

CONVENIENCE FOODS The range of convenience foods and ready-made dishes on the market is growing all the time, and is improving in quality. Using convenience foods doesn't make you a bad host. Frozen vegetables, ready-made soups and sauces, and pre-packed seasoning mixtures, used judiciously, can all be ingredients in a menu with a personal touch.

List of supplies

- Bread, rolls, crackers
- Milk, butter, curd or cottage cheese, cheese
- Rice
- Pasta
- Flour
- Eggs
- Oil
- Vinegar
- *Seasonings* Salt, sugar, pepper, paprika
- *Fresh vegetables* Tomatoes, sweet peppers, onions, garlic
- *Fresh fruit* Apples, bananas, oranges, lemons
- *Canned food* Meat, sausage, fish, vegetables, fruit
- Mineral water, fruit juices
- Coffee, tea, drinking chocolate
- Chocolate, sweet biscuits (cookies)

Setting the Table for a party

The meal is at the heart of a party, whether it is a buffet supper where the guests help themselves, or a dinner where eating together is the main event. In view of the formality that can be a feature of such dinners, however, many people steer clear of them. Fortunately ideas of good manners are more flexible these days. If you take a relaxed attitude to etiquette, you will find that you can give a party which is a real work of art and which all your guests enjoy – particularly when they sit down to the table.

Laying the table

THE TABLECLOTH The ideal tablecloth is white, but if the table decorations are colored or you are using china with a strong pattern, you can use any other color so long as it is not too dark. Always avoid black or very deep colors. The fabric of the cloth should be suitable for the meal; a damask tablecloth would be right for a sophisticated gourmet menu. It is always a good idea to place another soft, absorbent cloth between the table surface and the tablecloth proper, first to mute the sound as people put down their dishes and glasses, and second to mop up any liquids as soon as they are spilt.

The table setting

CHINA Dinner services are usually sold in sets for six to twelve people. If you often invite guests to dinner parties you should choose a plain design on the dinner service; then any breakages can be more easily replaced, and if you are giving a very large party you can supplement the basic china with borrowed plates, and the mixture will not be too obvious. The summer and winter sales that are held in big department stores or specialist china shops provide a very good opportunity to stock up for large parties. You can often be lucky and find a complete dinner service at a relatively low price in the sales.

The classic dinner service for six consists of:
• 6 cups (with saucers and breakfast plates)
• 6 large dinner plates
• 6 large soup plates (or soup bowls)
• 6 small side plates
• 6 small dessert plates
• 1 large dessert bowl
• 2 serving platters
• 2 vegetable dishes
• 1 coffee pot
• 1 teapot
• 1 sauceboat
• 1 milk jug
• 1 sugar bowl

The Menu
several delicious courses

In the past, celebrating an occasion with a festive meal used to mean placing all kinds of different dishes on the table simultaneously and eating them in any order. In France, as in Italy, where good food is an integral part of everyday life, it gradually became the custom to serve the individual components of a festive meal in a certain order – the idea of a menu was born. Step by step, the meal progresses through a range of hot and cold, sweet and savory dishes, culminating in the highlight of the meal, the main course, and finishing with a sweet dessert, fruit, or cheese.

Starters (Appetizers)

Amuse-gueules This somewhat unusual French term for appetizers means literally "something to tickle the palate" and would not normally feature on the menu. These clever little creations enable the chef to show off his skills. Anyone adept at such culinary arts can be sure of getting the meal off to a brilliant start. "Amuse-gueules" are normally served cold and can therefore be prepared well in advance.

Hot or cold starter The actual "first course" of a meal is generally a small dish in itself. A cold starter could consist of a tasty salad, a selection of ham or roast meats, fresh salmon or smoked trout, whereas a hot starter might be a meat- or fish-based dish. If you opt for a cold starter, it can be prepared in advance before the guests arrive.

Soup A light soup (not a hearty broth) can be served either as a hot starter or as a proper soup course. This, too, can be made in advance and be ready before the guests arrive.

Primo piatto In an Italian meal, it is at this stage that the famous pasta course is served, a "first dish" of pasta in sauce. Although the sauce can be prepared in advance, the pasta, if it is to be served "al dente", will require the full attention of the chef.

Main course

The central feature of the menu will be a meat, fish or poultry dish served with a vegetable accompaniment. For an intimate meal, a roast dish is ideal. It can be left to cook in the oven for several hours and then cut into slices when required. Fish and poultry can likewise be prepared using similar methods that save time. The accompanying vegetables

may be blanched – heated briefly in hot water – so that the host need spend only a short time in the kitchen.

Cheese

Cheese Two or three different types of cheese can be served with fresh bread and butter. Alternatively, a variety of soft cheeses may also be served.

Dessert Sweet dishes can likewise be served either hot or cold. Generally speaking, the favorites are ice cream and fruit-based dishes, such as fruit jelly (gelatine) or fruit salad, or a combination of the two. Cakes and tarts, pastries or other types of confectionery are also popular.

A Buffet
variety is the key

The first thing to decide when inviting guests is how the food is to be served. The type of meal outlined in the previous chapter would, in many ways, be reason enough for such an occasion. In a gathering of this type, "conversational skills" and the guest mix are of prime importance. At a traditional party, the food is, quite literally, peripheral, with the guests helping themselves to the various delicacies on offer and otherwise enjoying themselves, chatting and dancing.

The buffet selection at a glance

Basically, the arrangement of dishes at a buffet echoes a traditional menu. You start at one end of the buffet table with the starters (appetizers), to which the guests can help themselves according to preference. Next to these will be a selection of main course dishes, kept warm on hot plates. It is important to provide a little more than is actually needed – it is better for the host to be eating up leftovers for the next few days than for the food to start running out too early.

There need be no limits to your imagination when putting together a buffet meal. Unlike a specific menu, where the guest is tied to a prearranged series of dishes, a buffet is an ideal opportunity to try out unusual recipes. Any guest who is not partial to anything out of the ordinary can choose an alternative from the selection of dishes. You can also choose a particular theme for your buffet, for exam-

ple, an Oriental buffet, an "Arabian nights" buffet, or a buffet offering the increasingly popular American finger food. A buffet-style meal is perfect for brunch, where anything can be served, ranging from continental European-type breakfast dishes of croissants and jam to substantial meat, fish and poultry lunch dishes. Depending on each guest's internal clock, they can gradually progress from breakfast to lunch.

With a buffet, you do not require large plates, even for the main course, as the fun is in eating one's way through as many dishes as possible during the course of the party. That is why it is advisable to provide at least twice as many plates as there are guests. Washing dishes part way through poses something of a problem as no one wants to be hearing the clattering of dishes from the kitchen while they are eating. Desserts and cakes should be served on a separate table. If the size of the room or buffet table allows, cutlery and plates should be available at various locations.

Good Drinks
magic potions to set the mood

Just as important as the food are the drinks. The drinks to be served will depend on the guests and the menu. Expensive wines are more likely to be served at a festive dinner rather than at an informal party where there will be a greater demand for beer, cocktails and more modest wines. It is important to make sure that there is plenty of mineral water available as well as a selection of non-alcoholic beverages, such as fruit juices and soft drinks.

Aperitif

The question of which is the correct drink to serve before a meal or at the start of a buffet is a difficult one. The traditional French aperitifs are herbal schnapps with their acknowledged medicinal properties designed to prepare the digestive system for the demands about to be placed on it. Anglo-Saxon tastes favor sherry and vermouths, while Italians prefer a dry vermouth.

Cocktail

The making of cocktails, so-called because of their brightly colored ingredients, (derived from the English word meaning a "cockerel's tail") is a science in itself. Ambitious barkeepers compete in international competitions to find the most creative inventor of drink combinations. Even on a private level, however, given the necessary experience, you can give the most wonderful cocktail parties. A degree of caution should be exercised, however, when drinking cocktails with such fascinating names as "Planter's Punch", "Tequila Sunrise", "Bloody Mary" or "Pina Colada" as mixing spirits in this way can very quickly lead to inebriation.

Longdrinks

Longdrinks are much less costly to serve than cocktails and are ideal for a casual afternoon get-together, even as aperitifs. They consist, as a rule, of just two main ingredients: a high-proof spirit, such as gin, vodka or rum, topped up with a non-alcoholic mixer drink, such as tonic water, ginger ale or bitter lemon to make it "long".

Wine

Wine forms the perfect accompaniment to almost any meal. Which wine goes best with which food, however, remains a question of personal taste. Now that the last taboo of never drinking red wine with fish has been removed, it is more than ever a matter of individual preference. Anyone beginning to turn his attention to such matters will no doubt soon make his way to a reliable wine merchant or even the "local" vintner for some sound advice. Although buying wine is by no means an inexpensive business, it is not always the most expensive wine that is the best accompaniment to a meal.

As a rule of thumb, dry wines, which enhance the flavor of the food without overpowering it, make the best accompaniment to a meal. If a meal is so elaborate that it demands a succession of different types of wine during the various courses, then the finer wine should be served after the more modest

Basic requirements for the cocktail bar

- **Angostura**
- **Brandy**
- **Campari**
- **Fresh or preserved fruit**
- **Fruit juices**
- **Gin**
- **Ginger ale**
- **Grenadine syrup**
- **Liqueurs**
- **Olives**
- **Port**
- **Rum**
- **Soda water**
- **Tequila**
- **Tonic water**
- **Vermouth**
- **Vodka**
- **Whisky**

one and the heavier and richer wine should follow the lighter one.

The ideal temperature for white wine is 50–53°F (10–12°C) and 60–64°F (16–18°C) for red wine. (NB: The advice that red wine should be consumed at "room temperature" stems from the days when not all rooms were heated to 68°F [20°C]!). In the case of some older red wines, it is sometimes a good idea to decant them first, in other words, pour them out of the bottle into a carafe. This not only gives the long confined wine an injection of oxygen, but also means that any sediment is retained in the bottle.

Equipment for the cocktail bar

- **Bottle opener**
- **Can opener**
- **Chopping board**
- **Cocktail shaker**
- **Cocktail sticks**
- **Drinking straws**
- **Ice bucket**

- **Ice cubes**
- **Ice tongs**
- **Jugs (glass, metal)**
- **Mixers**
- **Slotted spoon**
- **Spoons (long-handled)**

Sparkling wine

"Sparkling wine" is the overall term given to any wine that undergoes a second fermentation and is bottled before fermentation is completely finished. Such wines sparkle or "effervesce". All German sparkling wines produced according to a specific procedure can be labelled "Sekt". The most sophisticated type of sparkling wine is champagne, which is made exclusively from grapes grown in the Champagne region. To be eligible for the "Champagne" label, the grapes must have followed a strictly prescribed fermentation process. German Sekt and Spanish Cava may also have the words "méthode champenoise" on the label if they have been processed in this way. Over the past years, it has become perfectly acceptable for the very dry versions of Sekt, Cava and Champagne, labelled "brut" or "extra brut", to be served throughout the entire meal. Sweeter varieties of Sekt or even sweet sparkling wines, for example Russian Crimean sparkling wine or Italian Spumante, are really only suitable as an aperitif or as an accompaniment to dessert.

Beer

Whether you are enjoying a simple meal of plain food or very spicy, exotic cuisine, beer makes a very pleasant companion. There are many varieties of the "amber nectar", as it is called, and despite all the attempts to centralize industrial beer production, a large number of local specialties still exist. These are often only discovered by seeking out small local breweries, in the same way that wine connoisseurs visit their favorite local winegrowers. Similarly, the best way to find out what you like is by tasting: choose between mild malt export beer, bitter hop-flavored Pils, sweet dark beer, strong lager-type beer from Cologne or light wheat (weiss) beer. Nowadays, supermarkets not only stock the current brands of North American, German and European beers, but also imports from Central America and Australia so that everything is available for an international beer party. Most of the major breweries produce canned beer and young people, in particular, regard cans of beer as "cool". Real beer fans, however, would eschew canned beer. There is more at stake here than fashion trends: In order to extend the life of canned beer, additional preservatives are added to it, which have an adverse effect on the flavor.

Spirits

The meal is rounded off with "spirits" intended to aid the digestive processes. Although the beneficial effects of high-proof alcoholic drinks are still a matter for debate in the medical world, this in no way diminishes the pleasure they afford. Every host should have a selection of brandy, fruit schnapps, clear corn schnapps, aquavit or grappa to offer his guests.

Music – a mixed blessing?

Whether or not to have music at a celebration is always a vexing question – what some people find enjoyable can to others be an intolerable source of irritation. If it is a party for close friends, it will be easy to find a type of music that is acceptable to everyone. If the guests include a lot of unknown faces, whose likes and dislikes are not known, then often a little goes a long way, especially since any additional background noise will mean an increase in the volume of conversation, making it difficult to hold a relaxed conversation. Depending on where you live, it is important to warn your immediate neighbors that you are planning to give a party.

Disc jockey or live music

Employing the services of a disc jockey or a band is certainly more fun than relying on CDs for music. Even though he himself can only play recorded music, a professional disc jockey will be able to cater for a far wider range of musical tastes than could be found in any average record collection. He should also have the ability to tune into the prevailing age of his audience. Having live artists at the event would certainly be something special, although the scope for this is very limited within your own home. Regardless of where the party is to be held, if you are going to include live entertainment, it is important to ask yourself the following questions:

- When will the show start and at what time will it finish?
- Is there a stage? If not, which part of the room is best suited for the band's performance?
- Are there lighting facilities available?

- Will the band need a soundcheck or other technical checks? If so, when can these be carried out?
- Will the band be bringing its own technical equipment or must this be provided?
- Are private changing room facilities available for the musicians and how will they reach the stage as unobtrusively as possible?

Background music

Musical entertainment does not always have to be provided by a dance band. For smaller gatherings, even a solo musician would be quite adequate. For an elegant dinner, soft background music could be provided by an experienced bar pianist or, if the host is feeling extravagant, a harpist. If you are contemplating live music at your event, you would do well to consult an artists' agency. These can be found in all major towns.

The right Outing
to suit every occasion

If the celebrations are to continue throughout the whole day, it may be a good idea to change venues at some point. You could, for example, arrange for lunch to be in the form of a picnic in the park, or include a stroll to a nearby beauty spot or tourist attraction prior to afternoon coffee. Particularly where children number among the guests, a little outing like this can make the day's program more exciting and less formal. If the party includes elderly people, however, you should gauge any activities requiring physical effort with them in mind.

Preparation is the key to success

Any excursion, like the entire celebration itself, requires thorough planning and preparation. It is imperative for anyone planning an occasion of this sort to take the time to do this early in the proceedings so as to avoid misjudging the tastes of the guests and possibly upsetting them as a result. This will help to avoid embarrassing situations. If you are planning a picnic in the park, for example, it is advisable to enquire beforehand whether you would indeed be permitted to organize a party there.

Should a restaurant be the ultimate destination of the outing for your guests, it is wise to reserve the appropriate number of seats or a special room well in advance. In this way, you will not end up standing with your guests in a busy café or restaurant where there is not enough seating for everyone. If you have it in mind to walk to your destination, you, as the host, would be well advised to try the route out yourself beforehand in order to check the condition of the path. It is important to remember how conditions can alter following a shower of rain. It is best to have a contingency plan ready for such an eventuality.

If you are planning to go somewhere by car, then the logistical aspects of this must be organized in advance. How many vehicles will be available with how many seats? Are all the car owners and drivers prepared to offer their services? If the party is going to finish at some outlying destination, there must be provision for all the guests to be returned to some central location. Might there be a rail connection nearby?

If the celebrations are to include an excursion, it is a good idea to give some thought well in advance as to the exact sequence of events. You do not, after all, want it to appear like a last-minute idea for filling the gap between meals. What places are there to visit in the vicinity in addition to the usual gastronomic attractions? Is there a zoo, perhaps, a botanical garden, an orangerie or a bird park in the neighborhood? An interesting ruined castle or a splendid palace? An unusual collection or an interesting museum? Can individual tours be arranged for your guests? Are any important or original sporting or cultural events being held in the area on the day of your party? Is there a river or a lake nearby where you might be able to charter a cruise boat for your entire party? If you look carefully around the area, you are likely to discover countless opportunities, both great and small, which might be incorporated into your program, thus adding variety and interest to the day's events.

10 golden rules for a successful party

There is no secret formula for preventing any unforeseen eventualities and making sure that no unexpected problems arise. There are, however, a few basic rules which require minimum effort and which will help to create a polite and respectful atmosphere between guest and host.

1. Setting a financial limit

The budget limit for a celebration can vary as much as the occasion itself. That is why it is a good idea to set a limit to your budget right at the outset. Depending on the number of guests, inviting people to a tea party is going to cost considerably less than a large party with professional live entertainment or a lavish ball. It is important, therefore, to decide the main requirements and calculate the cost as accurately as possible. If you work out your budget carefully, you will be able to see what may be discarded and what is indispensable for your particular occasion. In this way, you should then end up with something really good. One of the worst things that can befall you as a host is to be thought cheap.

2. Replying to an invitation

In the case of a formal invitation, the abbreviation "RSVP" requires the recipient to respond as soon as possible, saying whether he or she will be able, or unable, to attend the event. When replying, it is a good idea to add a few words of thanks and say that you are looking forward to the occasion. Even if, or perhaps particularly if, you have to decline the invitation, it is still important to reply. This should be done as early as possible, mentioning a specific reason why you have to decline and expressing a few words of regret.

3. Arriving punctually and not overstaying your welcome

Courtesy demands that you should arrive punctually, but "punctuality" can be a relative concept. In the case of dinner or a working lunch, it is very important to stick to the given time. If the event is a brunch or party, however, you can turn up even an hour after it has started without being thought unpunctual. In the case of an afternoon tea party, it is acceptable to arrive up to 15 minutes late, and up to half an hour late for a reception. Gauging the time of your departure requires a degree of sensitivity. Hearing your host good-naturedly call out "Right, let's just have one for the road" is definitely a polite hint that it is time to think about making your departure.

4. Choosing the right clothes for the occasion

As a general rule: the better the guests are dressed, the greater is their respect for the host and the occasion in question. On the other hand, it is considered impolite to outshine the host in terms of dress. Since there are so many types of celebrations nowadays, any host anxious lest his guests arrive too casually dressed for his occasion will mention the required dress code on the invitation: "Evening dress or dark suit please." "Smart casual" is also a good guide.

5. Switching off mobile phones

One of the most useful, yet at the same time irritating, technical advances in recent years is the mobile phone. As a general principle, these should be switched off in company. Any guests who have to remain contactable by phone, either for business reasons or because they are doctors on call, should inform the host at the outset and, in the event of an incoming call, withdraw discreetly. The same thing applies to the host. If the telephone rings, it is up to him to be as brief as possible and arrange a time to ring back later.

6. Choosing a gift for your host with a personal touch

There is no obligation to take a present along to a party or an invitation to dinner. The traditional present is a bouquet of flowers for the lady of the house. If some thought has been given to the gift and it has been specifically chosen with the recipient in mind, it can be a token of a good and strong relationship between the guest and his host. You cannot, however, turn up empty-handed for a birthday or wedding celebration. If you are not a member of the immediate family or a close friend, it might be advisable to ask around beforehand to find out what sort of present might be appropriate or acceptable. The Wedding or Bridal Registry set up in a household goods store or a department store, is becoming an increasingly common feature of weddings. The equipment on display there will have been chosen by the bridal couple and anyone wanting to contribute to the dinner service or kitchenware may do so. This may not be a particularly "personal gift" but at least the couple may be certain of getting a service of their own choice as a wedding present.

7. Keeping the speech short and sweet

The speeches at a special occasion can either lighten or ruin the atmosphere. The best time to give a speech is between two courses of a meal. In the case of a buffet, however, the opportune moment must be seized at an appropriate point in the proceedings. The speech should be kept as short and succinct as possible. If the host wishes to elect one of the guests to make a speech, this should be communicated to the guest well before the event so that the elected speaker can prepare something suitable. In choosing someone to speak at an event, it is important to consider not just that person's rhetorical skills but also how well he is acquainted with the host.

8. Steering a course between tact and taboo

One of the main reasons for getting together to celebrate an occasion is to communicate. As far as parties are concerned, "communicating" means talking, exchanging views, making conversation, small talk and gossip. The latter, however, is always a bit tricky since you never know whether the person you are talking to is acquainted with the person you are gossiping about. Generally speaking, gossiping about people behind their backs is frowned upon, no matter how much fun it may be. The same applies to the subject of illness, the second most popular topic of conversation after the weather. Nor should disparaging remarks be made about so-called "fringe groups" as another guest may easily feel provoked and a row could flare up. The hosts have a responsibility in this respect. Choosing your guests is just as important as introducing them to each other in such a way that everyone knows which subjects they can talk about to whom and which should be steered clear of.

9. Arranging overnight accommodation

If some of the guests have had to travel a fair distance, overnight accommodation must be arranged for them well in advance, making sure that couples and groups are not split up and older guests provided with the maximum comfort. Breakfast should also be provided if possible. If no or not enough guest rooms are available, other arrangements must be made for accommodating overnight guests. This may mean reserving hotel or bed and breakfast accommodation, or using the guest rooms of neighbors or close friends living in the vicinity. The cost of hotel accommodation should, of course, be met by the hosts.

10. Thanking your hosts for their hospitality

After a party, it is proper for guests to thank their hosts once again for their hospitality. This should be done one to three days afterwards in a handwritten note or by way of an informal telephone call, fax or e-mail. Similarly, the person whose birthday has been celebrated or the bridal couple should express their thanks for any gifts received. This is best done in writing, preferably in the form of a handwritten message on a tasteful card and mentioning the respective present.

Family parties

Make sure those occasions for family celebration turn into wonderful memories

A party for all occasions:
The family party

Sometimes there seems no reason to have a party; Christmas and Easter are far away, everybody in the family of marriageable age has already exchanged vows, and there are no big birthdays in sight. For those who feel decisive and are not afraid of the work involved, why not invite all the family to a party "just because"? The idea is certain to appeal to one and all.

An ideal theme for a family party is "a feast in the country". The best time is the late summer when everyone has returned from his or her holidays, the fruits to be used for the decoration and the food have been harvested. A party like this needs a bit of space – apart from the indoor rooms there should be room to have the party outside if the weather permits. Amusing games and hearty food are now the important thing. Along with a substantial goulash soup and an artistically constructed mountain of herb cheese and radishes, the main course on the buffet is delicious knuckle of veal. The cheese and leek baguettes go wonderfully well with the cider punch. To round everything off nicely there is a simple chocolate cake. Later in the evening you will be able to lose the pounds you have just gained by dancing to foot-tapping music.

TABLE AND BUFFET The buffet is set up using rural themes. A motif for the tablecloths and napkins could be cows or geese, but a rustic checkered pattern is also suitable. You will find a large selection in department stores or material shops. The plates can be simple white crockery that everyone will have at home. Bouquets of wild flowers and grasses make perfect centerpieces.

DECORATION The rural theme is not restricted to the table, but should be echoed in all the rooms in which the party is being held. Daisies, buttercups and any other wild flowers are perfect decorations. Agricultural implements such as milk churns, cowbells and milking stools will delight the guests and will round off the rustic atmosphere.

INVITATIONS The rural theme can be carried over to the invitation cards. You will need a piece of white cardboard the same size as a normal sheet of paper. Fold it in the middle. Using carbon paper, copy an enlarged version of the illustration of a cow onto the left side of the card and write your invitation on the right. There is no limit to your imagination when coloring the sketch.

Admittance to the Christian community

Children take part in a variety of religious festivals as they grow to adulthood. Different feasts are celebrated, depending on whether people are Roman Catholic or Protestant.

Confirmation in Anglican circles symbolizes the start of unrestricted membership of the church. Young people decide to attend confirmation classes and are allowed to take communion for the first time. This is a time of special celebration for those involved and the extravagance of the proceedings are designed to mirror this. Catholic confirmation reflects the same idea.

Acceptance into the Catholic community takes place in two stages. After children have participated in lessons about the mass for about six months, they are allowed to partake of the eucharist. This happens symbolically at what is known as "first communion." The festival was traditionally celebrated on the first Sunday after Easter. In recent years it has become more normal to celebrate this festival some time in May or June, not least because of the weather. Girls wear a white dress and a garland in their hair for this occasion, and boys wear a black suit. Children traditionally carry their birth candle during the ceremony.

The second important festival for young people is confirmation. During this ceremony, the bishop or authorized priest puts his hands on the candidates and speaks words of encouragement to them.

HINT More and more people are deciding to eat less meat, or are even deciding to become vegetarian altogether. A considerate host will take this into account when planning a menu. Most people know the likes and dislikes of the members of their own family, but if the occasion is to be somewhat "public", where the family will be inviting friends, colleagues or fiancées, then it is advisable to find out if there are any vegetarians among them. The theme "a feast in the country" in itself offers many possibilities for serving interesting and delicious vegetable dishes. This means there is truly something for every taste.

tip
Cooking the garlic in its peel flavors the cooking oil and leaves you with a tender, roasted clove inside. Eat it with the steak or spread it on toast for a quick, delicious hors d'oeuvre.

steak with cauliflower and crispy bread crumbs
hands-on time: 25 minutes | total time: 25 minutes | serves 4

1 small loaf French or Italian bread, torn into small pieces (about 2 cups)

3 tablespoons olive oil

2 tablespoons roughly chopped fresh flat-leaf parsley

1 tablespoon capers, roughly chopped

6 cloves garlic, unpeeled

1½ pounds strip steak

½ teaspoon kosher salt

½ teaspoon black pepper

1 head cauliflower, cut into florets

Heat oven to 400° F. Toss the bread in a bowl with 1½ tablespoons of the olive oil. Arrange in a single layer on a baking sheet. Bake until slightly golden and crispy, about 6 minutes. Transfer to a bowl and toss with the parsley and capers; set aside. Meanwhile, heat the remaining oil and the garlic in a large skillet (preferably cast-iron) over medium-high heat. Season the steak with the salt and pepper and cook until browned, 2 minutes per side. Transfer the steak to a baking dish and roast to the desired doneness, 6 to 8 minutes for medium-rare. Let rest at least 4 minutes before slicing. Add the cauliflower and ½ cup water to the skillet and cook, covered, until the cauliflower is tender and the water has evaporated, about 7 minutes. Divide the steak, cauliflower, and garlic among individual plates. Spoon the bread crumb mixture over the top.

THE
GREATEST
THING
SINCE SLICED BREAD
IS A
REPLACEMENT
FOR SLICED BREAD.

With the great taste of a bagel and the softness of bread, Thomas' Squares Bagelbread and new Thomas' Mini Squares Bagelbread are the best way to make a better sandwich.

Mini   Regular

PART BAGEL. PART BREAD. TOTALLY DELICIOUS.

M e n u

Strawberry punch with white rum

Cider punch

Goulash soup

Creamy herb cheese with radishes

Spicy herb and almond tart

Cheese and leek baguette

Farmer's salad

Knuckle of veal with mushrooms
and courgettes (zucchini)

Chocolate cake with yoghurt

Strawberry punch with white rum

Preparation time: 5 minutes, plus time for cooling

800 g/1¾ lbs strawberries

1 lemon

6 cl/2 fl oz (¼ cup) strawberry syrup

6 cl/2 fl oz (¼ cup) white rum

1 bottle alcoholic cider (chilled)

1 bottle dry sparkling wine (chilled)

❶ Wash the strawberries, trim and cut in half or quarters. Cut the lemons in half, squeeze the juice and pour over the strawberries. Stir in the strawberry syrup and white rum. Pour in the chilled cider. Leave in a cool place.

❷ Before serving fill up with the chilled sparkling wine.

Cider punch

Preparation time: 5 minutes, plus time for cooling

1 kg/2¼ lbs apples

10 cl/3 fl oz (⅓ cup plus 1½ table-spoons) lime juice

6 cl/2 fl oz (¼ cup) Amaretto

6 cl/2 fl oz (¼ cup) almond syrup

1 bottle alcoholic cider (chilled)

1 bottle dry sparkling wine (chilled)

❶ Wash the apples, quarter and remove the cores. Cut into small pieces, put in a bowl and mix with the lime juice. Add the Amaretto, almond syrup and the chilled cider. Leave the apples to steep for 3–4 hours.

❷ Fill up with the chilled sparkling wine just before serving.

HINT Make sure that along with baskets of bread, baguette and rolls there are also enough small pots of butter on the buffet.

For he's a jolly good fellow
The birthday party

It happens to each one of us every year and everyone deals with it in a different way. Some prefer a quiet day, perhaps so that there is nothing to remind them that they are growing older, or perhaps because they do not see growing older as of much significance or cause for celebration. However, many tend to "let rip" if the birthday is a round one as these birthdays represent symbolic milestones in life, and there is a world of difference if one is turning 20, 40 or 80. Every form of celebration can be held, from a dinner for one to a mega party or a festive ball.

For this reason we would like to offer two suggestions for an "everyday birthday party" at which several old friends can simply get together.

"JOURNEY THROUGH EUROPE" For the invitations, draw or copy a map of Europe. Each guest or couple are given a country and the present they bring – a bottle would be suitable in this case – should represent the country they have been given. Those who draw Spain, for instance, could appear as a pair of flamenco dancers carrying a bottle of sangria. The "Greeks" could wrap themselves in classical robes and have a bottle of ouzo with them as a digestif. You could even have a competition with prizes for the best costume.

The food should reflect the international theme of the party. Light starters (appetizers) from the Mediterranean, fiery dishes from the south-eastern part of the continent, ingenious delicacies from France and hearty dishes from Germany and Scandinavia would make an appetizing buffet. The tablecloths could be the national flags, which can be found in department and furniture stores or painted onto white cloths, instead of the white tablecloths which are generally the most advisable. Decorating the walls with newspapers from the different countries – which you can find at the airport or train station – will lend an international flair to the proceedings.

GOURMET FONDUE A fondue is a stylish way to celebrate the start of a new year in your life. After a small appetizer the guests choose between a fondue *Chinoise* – using broth – and the classic fondue *Bourguignonne*. Four fondue sauces and a vitamin-rich and crunchy salad will round off the variety of flavors. After the enjoyable meal there is a delightful sweet dessert to look forward to. As the room on the table will be limited due to the two rechauds and the many little sauce dishes, a simple

and symmetrical Asian style of decoration would be the most advisable. For this the table is divided into quarters with two lengths of bright red satin, about 10 cm/2 in wide. In each of the table halves two more strips of satin (about 40 x 10 cm/16 x 4 in) are laid across each other. This cross marks the spot where the rechaud will go. This strict geometrical decoration which allows one to concentrate completely on the flavor of the food can be enhanced by placing pebbles in patterns and single red blossoms in white vases.

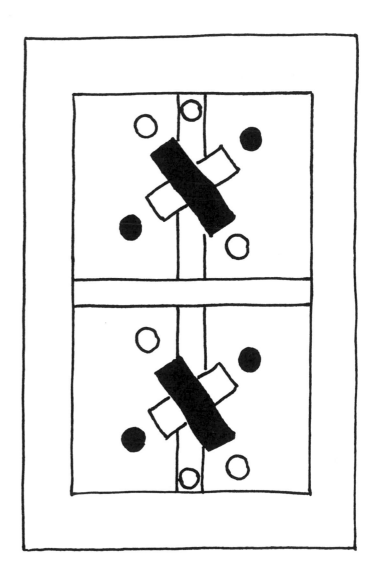

Demons drive out the dark powers

There was a great deal of resistance to celebrating birthdays for a long time in both the Jewish and Christian religions. Birthdays are not mentioned in the Bible and both the Jewish and Christian religions viewed these celebrations as idolatrous. This attitude led to the later Catholic custom of celebrating a person's name day rather than their real birthday. The reason given for this is still that nobody knows the exact date of Jesus' birth.

The ancient Greek world, however, believed that each person had a protecting spirit or demon which was present at their birth and guarded their protegé's life. People also believed that a mystical relationship existed between this spirit or demon and the god on whose birthday the person was born. Celebrating a person's birthday strengthened the link between the person, his or her protective spirit and the god in question and at the same time drove out evil powers.

The Romans adopted these ideas from the Greeks and developed a real cult on a person's birthday. The Greeks were already accustomed to offering honey cakes on the altars of the goddess Artemis. These were round like the moon and were decorated with burning candles. This custom still remains in our birthday celebrations, which have long since become part of our culture, despite Christian traditions.

The type of celebration varies greatly depending on the age of the person. For young children, the number of presents is often more important than the actual celebration, which frequently takes place in a kindergarten or is organized by a catering firm.

When people get older, birthday cards, flowers and small gifts from colleagues, friends and relatives play a more important role. Adults tend to celebrate birthdays divisible by ten in special ways. Many people treat themselves to something special and go on a journey or put on a lavish celebration with friends. These birthdays are often celebrated with large numbers of people gathering in a pub or professional catering services are called in and a hall is hired for the purpose.

Birthdays in Britain are celebrated in a variety of ways. Quite often close relatives or friends will make some kind of a speech, which may or may not include a poem or a song specially composed for the occasion.

People who are organizing a birthday celebration have to take many factors into account. Will people be able to travel to the celebration? Does it clash with holidays or other events which might take priority over people's ability to attend?

The place where the birthday is being celebrated is also important. If things are likely to turn rather wild, people tend to hire a hall rather than see their own property damaged. And, of course, if people have a birthday in the summer, barbecues in the garden are an ideal way of marking the occasion, weather permitting!

Menu

Coral champagne

Salmon reels on pumpernickel

Oil, broth, meat and vegetables for the fondues

Chicken broth for fondue *Chinoise*

Fondue *Bourguignonne*

Cognac and tomato sauce

Curry sauce

Cream cheese with cucumber and garlic

Mustard remoulade

Gardener's salad with pistachios

Mango mousse

Per glass

2 cl (1 tablespoon) gin

2 cl (1 tablespoon) campari

2 cl (1 tablespoon) vermouth

ice cubes

**200 ml/7 fl oz (¾ cup) dry champagne
or sparkling wine (chilled)**

Coral champagne

Preparation time: 5 minutes

Pour the gin, campari and vermouth into a champagne glass. Add the ice cubes and fill with the chilled champagne.

**50 g/1¾ oz (3½ tablespoons) soft
butter**

1 tablespoon grated horseradish

2 tablespoons chopped dill

salt

**3 slices smoked salmon (about
20 cm/8 in each)**

20 small rounds of pumpernickel

1 bunch dill

Salmon reels
on pumpernickel

Preparation time: 15 minutes

❶ Mix the butter with the horseradish and the dill, season with salt. Spread the slices of salmon with the marinade and roll up from the end.

❷ Cut the salmon into 1 cm/½ in thick reels (rolls) and lay on the rounds of pumpernickel. Wash the bunch of dill, pat dry and use to garnish the reels (rolls).

Classic fondue

When making the classic fondue, calculate about 200 g/7 oz meat for each person. Fondue *Bourguignonne* (the frying of cubes of beef) can of course be made with other meat such as lamb, pork or chicken. The main thing is that the meat is of the best quality.

Broth for the fondue
Chinoise

The broth should be fairly light to start with as it will get stronger as the meat and vegetables are cooked in it. You can add boiling water or a basic broth at the table as the meal progresses. Do not season the meat until after the cooking as it will otherwise become tough. Along with a salad there should always be enough baguette or little party rolls available.

A bond for life
The wedding

The alternative to a party lasting several days to which you invite all your relatives, acquaintances and friends would be to do exactly the opposite: just to invite as many people as fit comfortably around your dining room table and to spend the big day with close friends and family. There are no hard and fast rules for the invitations. The bridal couple will decide who will be amongst the chosen few. However, it is important on this day of all days that the guests get along well together.

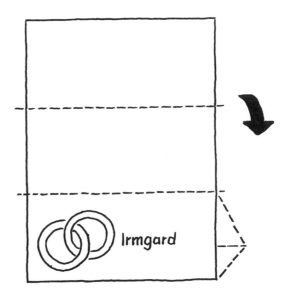

The festive dinner for up to eight people is of course the main theme at this intimate party – to invite more than this to a seated dinner at one table is rarely a good idea. Serving a champagne cocktail will get things off to a good start. This is followed by the classic five-course dinner which can be rounded off by a refreshing lime sherbet and a selection of cheeses.

DECORATIONS The basis of the table decorations is a white damask tablecloth. In keeping with the occasion and beneficial to the atmosphere are delicate and transparent silk materials in a soft pink. Square pieces of material about 50 cm (20 in) to a side are rolled into lengths and laid along the table. As the rose is the flower of lovers, it will predominate in the form of artistic but easily made wreaths.

You will need:
• 4 wreath rings (24–26 cm/9½–10 in diameter)
• moss
• trails of ivy
• wire
• 16 white roses
• 16 pink roses

First of all wrap the moss and the ivy around the wreath ring and fasten with the wire. Cut the stems off the roses just under the blossom leaving enough to wind a piece of wire around. The end of the wire is used to stick into the wreath. It is important to space the roses evenly around the ring. To keep the wreaths fresh it is advisable to put them into plates of water and to sprinkle with water occasionally.

A wedding dinner, even a small one in which most guests will probably have met before, is still a good opportunity to use place cards. These can be made using white cards, about 10 x 14 cm (4 x 5½ in) cored in the middle and folded back. Glue two entwined rings on to the front of the card and write

the guest's name. Depending on your artistic talent and the software on your PC, you can also make menu cards on which the courses as well as the occasion, place and date can be noted. This means that after the party your guests can take home a tasteful souvenir to remind them of this special day. The invitations – which must be sent out well in advance – can also contain a personal touch of your own. For this you need more white card, this time in writing paper size, which is folded in the middle. Attach two golden rings with silk thread to the left-hand side and write the invitation on the right-hand side. You can buy gold-colored rings in DIY markets and handicraft shops.

Dear Irmgard and Steven,

We would like to invite you to a small wedding party on the 4th September. Please come at 7.30pm bringing hearty appetites and good cheer with you.

Wedding traditions

A number of traditions have sprung up in connection with wedding days, the celebration many people would view as the most important day of their lives. In recent years many people feel that the subject of marriage has been so trivialised and commercialised that they are happy to revive ancient traditions. People either opt for a registry office wedding or a church celebration.

But before couples arrive at the altar, they make sure they enjoy the last few hours of single life. In Britain, men organise a stag party, an excuse for a booze-up among the lads. The ladies opt for a hen party, the last chance for the would-be bride to gather her companions around her and talk together.

The wedding breakfast takes place following the ceremony at the registry office or in church. People normally go to a restaurant or hire a hall where caterers provide the food and drink. In the Middle Ages there were laws prohibiting too much resplendence at weddings. For example it was forbidden to celebrate for longer than seven days and to give people more than forty meals!

Dress tends to be conservative. The ladies wear elegant dresses and often hats, while the men don suits. The bride wears a white veil and dress, symbols of her virginity and purity, and it is quite usual for the bridegroom and best man to wear morning dress, consisting of a tailed coat and striped trousers and a British bowler hat. However, in the past women did sometimes wear black. All kinds of superstitions surround a person's wedding day. The bridegroom is not supposed to see his bride prior to the ceremony and brides often wear a horseshoe to give them good luck. In other countries the bride is supposed to hide a coin in her shoe to ensure that the marriage will be prosperous. Or the bridegroom is not supposed to drive the wedding car, or the relationship might be bedevilled with bad luck.

On the day of the wedding the bride should follow the old adage and wear "something old, something new, something borrowed, something blue."

M e n u

Champagne cocktail

Grape and cheese appetizer

Mushroom soup with pastry lid

Salmon with green asparagus sauce

Lime sherbet

Stuffed turkey steaks
on a bed of potatoes with broccoli

Panna cotta with rhubarb compote

Champagne cocktail

Preparation time: 5 minutes

❶ Chill the glasses.

❷ Put the sugar cube in the glass. First pour in the Angostura Bitters, then the cognac. Fill with champagne, garnish with a slice of orange.

Per glass

1 sugar cube

1 dash Angostura Bitters

3 cl/1fl oz (2 tablespoons) cognac

14 cl/4¾ fl oz (⅔ cup) champagne (chilled)

orange slices for garnishing

Grape and cheese appetizer

Preparation time: 20 minutes

❶ Wash the grapes and remove the seeds. Mix the cream cheese with the cream and sweet basil, season to taste with salt and pepper.

❷ Toast the almond flakes in a frying pan, allow to cool and then grind.

❸ Cover each individual grape with cream cheese and roll in the toasted almonds. Arrange on two plates.

500 g/1 lb grapes

400 g/14 oz cream cheese

1 tablespoon single (whipping) cream

1 tablespoon chopped sweet basil

salt

freshly ground pepper

100 g/3½ oz almond flakes

Mushroom soup
with pastry lid

Preparation time: 45 minutes

❶ Clean the mushrooms, wipe with kitchen paper (paper towles) and cut into thin slices. Peel the onions and chop finely.

❷ Heat the butter in a pot and brown the onions. Add the mushrooms, cover and cook for about 10 minutes.

❸ Peel the garlic, press and add to the mushrooms. Pour in the white wine. Add the broth, crème fraîche and cream. Stir the soup well and season with lemon juice, salt and pepper to taste. Stir in the parsley and put somewhere cool.

❹ Defrost the puff pastry according to the instructions on the packet, cut the pieces in half and roll out. According to the number of guests, cut out 6–8 rounds. The rounds must be at least 1 cm (½ in) larger than the soup bowls.

❺ Separate the egg yolk from the white. Brush the edges of the soup bowls and the pastry with the egg white. Pour in the soup. Put on the lid of pastry and press firmly to the edge of the bowl. Pre-heat the oven to 200°C, 400°F, gas mark 6.

❻ Brush the pastry lids with the egg yolk. Put the bowls in the pre-heated oven and bake until the pastry is crisp. Serve immediately.

HINT Ladle the soup into the bowls so that there is still 2–3 cm (1–1¼ in) room between the soup and the lid. It is particularly important that the soup is completely cooled before putting on the pastry lids, otherwise they will collapse.

500 g/1 lb mushrooms

1 onion

50 g/1¾ oz (3½ table spoons) butter

1 clove of garlic

100 ml/3 fl oz (½ cup) white wine

100 ml/3¼ fl oz (½ cup) instant chicken broth

200 ml/6¾ fl oz crème fraîche

375 ml/12½ fl oz (1½ cups) single (whipping) cream

2 teaspoons lemon juice

salt

freshly ground pepper

2 tablespoons chopped parsley

800 g/1¾ lb puff pastry (deep frozen)

1 egg

Salmon with green asparagus sauce

Preparation time: 40 minutes

1 kg/2¼ lbs green asparagus

salt

2 cartons single (whipping) cream

4 tablespoons crème fraîche

200 ml/6¾ fl oz (¾ cup) dry white wine

freshly ground white pepper

8 salmon steaks (about 200 g/7 oz each)

juice from 1 lemon

400 ml/13½ fl oz (1⅔ cups) vegetable broth

❶ Wash the asparagus, cut off the woody ends. Cook in boiling salted water for 15–20 minutes – it should still be crisp – remove from the water and drain.

❷ Heat the cream and whisk to a creamy sauce with the crème fraîche and the wine. Season with salt and pepper, add the asparagus.

❸ Heat the vegetable broth, sprinkle the salmon with lemon juice and put in the hot broth for 6–8 minutes.

❹ Take the salmon out of the broth and serve with the asparagus sauce.

Lime sherbet

Preparation time: 20 minutes

100 g/3½ oz sugar

250 ml/8¾ fl oz (1 cup) freshly squeezed lime juice

1 egg white

❶ Boil the sugar with 50 ml/1½ fl oz (3½ tablespoons) water for exactly 5 minutes. Allow the syrup to cool and mix with the lime juice.

❷ Put the syrup in the freezer and allow to almost freeze. Beat the egg white and fold in to the syrup. Return to freezer, taking out often and stirring vigorously so that the sherbet does not become hard.

❸ Take out of the freezer about 30 minutes before serving and stir.

HINT A sherbet is a fruity entrée (appetizer) that offers an exquisite transition to the flavor of the main course. Sherbets made of raw fruit juices – without using a sherbet machine – can be made 2–3 days before the party. Sherbets can also be made with vegetable purée or flower essences.

The typical agenda of a large wedding party with family and friends depends on the time of the wedding in the church or registry office (city hall) and could look like this:

- marriage ceremony
- champagne reception
- lunch, with speeches
- afternoon coffee with cakes
- dinner
- entertainment with dancing and contributions from either professional artists or from the guests

Depending on the professional and social background and on the originality and creativity of the bridal couple, the festivities can take place in almost any imaginable place. As with all other parties, there are practically no restrictions as to where and how you decide to celebrate the occasion. The traditional place for a party, however, is in one of the homes of the two families – be it the home of the new couple, or of one of the sets of parents. Here some preparation is necessary regarding the decoration of the tables and the buffet.

TABLES AND BUFFET The base of the buffet is made with two or three large boards made of chipboard (about 180 x 80 cm/72 x 32 in and 30 mm/1½ in thick). These are laid over trestles and covered with tablecloths or nice sheets that hang to the floor. Afterwards, white tulle is sewn to a curtain band so that it falls in folds and this is then stapled to the top edge of the table. The length of 80–100 cm/32–40 in-wide tulle needed will be twice the circumference of the table. As an example: a table of 180 x 80 cm/72 x 32 in has a circumference of 5.2 m/17 ft 4 in. Therefore you would need a length of tulle of 10.4 m/34 ft 8 in for one table.

For a table decoration made of bowers of flower garlands you will need (depending on the number

HINT Because the moss is damp the flowers stay fresh for almost a week. It is best, however, not to use flowers that are already too fully open. Sprinkle occasionally with water.

and size of the tables):
- florist's wire
- parcel string
- damp moss
- gypsophila (baby's breath)
- roses of all kinds
- trails of ivy

Shorten the stalks of the roses, the baby's breath and the ivy all to 14 cm/5½ in. Tie together to make little firm bouquets. Lay the parcel string out double and cut to the required length. Tie the moss to the string using the wire and not leaving any gaps. Now lay all the little bouquets facing in the same direction and tie them on with wire also. Arrange the garlands down the middle of the individual tables in a winding pattern.

TABLE DECORATIONS In order to make sure that the bridal couple really are on "cloud 9", the tables should be decorated with clouds you can make yourself. Transfer the pattern onto carbon paper, enlarge somewhat and transfer again to light blue construction paper which can then be cut out. Glue blue satin ribbons to the clouds and fasten them to the tulle with safety pins.

INVITATIONS When making the invitation cards you can follow the same procedure as when making the table decorations. Cut out the little clouds and write your invitation on them.

WEDDING CUSTOMS

When the couple emerge from the ceremony, they are often bombarded with confetti, an old custom which derives from the urge to drive away evil spirits. In Germany, children disperse flower petals, which are supposed to make people fruitful. There is also a centuries-old tradition of making a lot of noise: tin cans are attached to the rear of the couple's car, but once more, the reason is the same: people saw the need to drive away evil spirits.

The couple are expected to cut the wedding cake holding the knife together, as a sign of their new joint life. Some say that the person with their hand on top will have the last word in the marriage. In other countries it is common to have a large loaf of bread on the table, which is supposed to be distributed to the poor.

Or in Germany it is common for the bride to be carried away during the celebrations. The poor bridegroom then has the task of tracking his lady down.

Speeches play a major role at British weddings. It is customary for the bride's father to open these proceedings after the meal is over. He tends to speak lovingly but humorously about his daughter. This is followed by the bridegroom, who thanks people for all the hard work they have put into organizing the celebrations. He also customarily uses the "we" form for the first time with reference to his wife and himself.

The final speech comes from the bridegroom's best man who proposes a toast to the bridesmaids. But before doing so, he attempts to reveal the true colours of the man who has just married his wife. The best man is expected to speak in a very humorous manner.

Menu

Sherry cocktail

Tuna rolls

Potato soup with watercress

Shrimp and curry salad

Fish on a bed of vegetables

Roast lamb with herb crust, green sauce
and creamy herb dip

Orange cream cake

Strawberry quark cream

Sherry cocktail

Preparation time: 3 minutes

❶ Put all the ingredients into a shaker and shake well. Crush the ice cubes, add to the shaker and shake again.

❷ Pour the sherry cocktail through a sieve (strainer), remove the ice and serve.

2 cl (1 tablespoon plus one teaspoon) dry sherry

2 cl (1 tablespoon plus one teaspoon) red vermouth

1 cl (2 tablespoons) Spanish liqueur

1 cl (2 tablespoons) campari

2–3 ice cubes

Tuna rolls

Preparation time: 60 minutes

❶ Drain the tuna, mash with a fork and purée with the cream cheese. Wash the basil, pat dry and cut the leaves into thin strips. Cut the olives into small pieces. Stir the basil and the olives into the tuna purée and mix everything well. Season to taste with salt, pepper and paprika.

❷ Peel the onions and cut into thin rings. Cut the rolls in half. Spread the tuna purée on each half and garnish with onions rings. Sprinkle with paprika powder.

700 g/25 oz tuna in oil (tinned/canned)

500 g/1 lb cream cheese

1 bunch sweet basil

100 g/3½ oz black olives (pitted)

salt

freshly ground pepper

paprika powder

2 onions

18 fresh bread rolls

Potato soup with watercress

Preparation time: 1 hour, 15 minutes

❶ Peel the potatoes and cut into large cubes. Peel the onions and chop finely. Heat the oil in a pot and sauté the potatoes and onions until transparent. Add the broth, cover and simmer everything for about 25 minutes.

❷ Cut the stalks off the watercress carefully with a pair of scissors. Purée together with the cream.

❸ Purée the soup. Fold in the cress-cream and the horseradish and heat up again. Season with salt, pepper, some Tabasco, lemon juice and sugar.

2½ kg potatoes

1 large onion

4 tablespoons olive oil

3 liters/5½ pints (12 cups) vegetable broth (instant)

500 g/1 lb watercress

400 ml/13½ fl oz (1⅔ cups) single (whipping) cream

3 tablespoons horseradish

salt

freshly ground pepper

Tabasco sauce

3 tablespoons lemon juice

1 pinch sugar

The very first party
The christening

In earlier times, because of the high mortality rate among children, most christenings were held as soon as possible after a child was born. Today, many parents like to wait until the child is old enough to be more conscious of being accepted into the arms of the church. Whenever it may be celebrated, it is a particularly solemn occasion of great personal and social significance alike.

HINT Friends and acquaintances of couples who have just had a baby are usually in a similar age-group and situation. This means that they may also have small children who should not be left out of the festivities when you are celebrating your own child's christening. However, planning a party including a large number of children of all ages from new-born through primary school does pose a special challenge. The dinner should not be so formal that the children become bored. Perhaps it is possible to have a separate dining room for them. Then games could be organized for the small guests after they have eaten. As the hostess and her child should not be subjected to undue stress, it might be advisable to think well in advance about baby-sitters and children's entertainers. These could be hired professionals or perhaps recruited from the ranks of relatives and acquaintances.

The christening is one of the largest family parties that offers the chance of combining the cocktail party with a five-course dinner. The agenda for this special day depends – as is the case with a wedding party – on the time that the church service takes place. As the mother and child are the central figures in this celebration it is important that they are looked after and that the party is planned around their needs. When making preparations this means that the food has to be prepared well in advance so that it can have the finishing touches added and be served without too much fuss.

Those who would like to avoid this altogether, can, of course, hire a catering service who will relieve them of all worries with regard to the food.

DECORATIONS If the one to be christened is still a baby, the table decorations can pick up on this theme and use the motifs birth and baby. As usual, the foundation is a white tablecloth decorated with pink or blue satin (depending on whether the child is a girl or a boy). Colored ribbons in the same color are run through the rings on dummies (pacifiers) and fastened to the tablecloth with safety pins at regular intervals. Small flowering sprigs from a box-tree (that the florist can color for you) make the flower arrangements.

For breaks between the service and the dinner or even between the courses, games are a good idea. However, these need to be well-planned in advance. When sending the invitations, ask your guests to bring their own baby pictures with them. They should hand these in at the door on arrival. Later the photos are handed around and everybody has to guess which guest belongs to which baby photo.

MENU CARDS For the hand-written menu cards you will need pieces of thick, white, shiny card 15 x 22 cm/6 x 8½ in. Score in the middle and fold so that you have a folding card of 15 x 11 cm/6 x 4¼. With a gold pen write the menu on the right-hand side and on the outside you can glue a picture – if you have one – of the baby to be christened.

Menu

Blessing and protection for a new member of the human race

Even parents who have nothing to do with the church often want their child to be baptized. They feel the need to provide blessing and protection for their newly arrived offspring in a visible ceremony. They also want to celebrate the safe arrival of their child. Many traditions dictate how the celebration is organized. In the past, one thing was paramount: baptisms had to take place quickly to ensure the child did not die without being baptized.

Baptisms in Germany and Britain are normally celebrated by a small number of people. In the USA, however, large numbers of people gather. More and more young people now tend to invite not only their relatives but also friends. This means there are often many young children at these celebrations. So these occasions are no longer celebrated by people eating a set meal – informality is now the order of the day.

In the Anglo-Saxon world, the white baptismal dress is often an ancient family heirloom which is handed down from one generation to another. Sometimes all the names of the children who have already worn it are embroidered in the material. Other families make the baptismal dress from material from the mother's wedding dress or use the bride's veil to cover the cushion in which the baby is held. The child's name and its date of birth are marked on the baptismal candle. Sometimes friends or godparents make the candle themselves and add their good wishes for the child being baptized or explain the meaning of the child's name. In Anglo-Saxon countries it is relatively normal for the child to be not just sprinkled with holy water but actually placed in the water. Easter Eve is considered an especially festive and suitable date for baptisms in the Catholic Church to mark this first celebration for the young baby.

Friends of the parents often set up a kind of Maypole in the garden in Germany and hang children's clothes and babies' toys on it. Or a wooden stork suddenly appears in the garden carrying pink or light blue shoes in its beak, depending on the baby's sex. Other people hang the shoes on the front door to let other people know about the new arrival.

Baptism in the Anglican and Roman Catholic churches signifies acceptance into the Christian family. Confirmation, on the other hand, marks the teenagers' acceptance as fully adult church members. The ceremony is aimed at reinforcing their faith. This celebration tends to be celebrated in small gatherings, mainly in churches, both in Germany and Anglo-Saxon countries. The service often takes place on a weekday because the bishop conducting the ceremony is not able to attend the church on a Sunday. In the old days, confirmation day was often the first occasion when teenagers wore a dark suit. But things are no longer so rigid. The children are the centre of attention and are allowed to decide how they would like to celebrate. But it largely remains a celebration marking the transition from childhood to adulthood. For this reason many young people choose an "adult" setting for a meal – and grown-up clothes.

M e n u

Apple and raspberry drink

Terlaner wine soup
with cinnamon croutons

Salad hearts with vinaigrette

Loin of veal

Green beans with lemon sauce

Tea towel (dish towel) dumpling

Bavarian cream

Apple and raspberry drink with rum

Preparation time: 10 minutes

500 g/1 lb organic apples

2 tablespoons raspberries

1 unsprayed lemon

juice from ½ lemon

16 cl/5½ (⅔ cup) rum

❶ Wash the apples thoroughly and cut into quarters. Wash the raspberries and pick over.

❷ Using a juice extractor, juice the apples and the raspberries and pour into eight glasses.

❸ Wash the lemon thoroughly and cut into eight pieces. Decorate the rims of the glasses with these. Season the apple and raspberry drink with lemon juice and add the rum.

Terlaner wine soup with cinnamon croutons

Preparation time: 15 minutes

3 stale rolls

30 g (2 tablespoons) butter

1 pinch cinnamon

750 ml/25 fl oz (3 cups) instant
   chicken broth

5 egg yolks

200 ml/7 fl oz (¾ cup) single
   (whipping) cream

200 ml/7 fl oz (¾ cup) white wine

❶ Cut the bread rolls into cubes. Heat the butter in a pan and fry the cubes until golden brown and crisp. Season lightly with cinnamon.

❷ Beat the chicken broth with the egg yolks, cream, white wine and cinnamon until creamy. Do not allow to boil as otherwise the egg yolk will curdle.

❸ Sprinkle the hot cinnamon croutons over the soup and serve.

Salad hearts with vinaigrette

Preparation time: 30 minutes

500 g/1 lb head lettuce hearts (or 2 heads of lettuce)

2 tablespoons wine vinegar

herb salt

freshly ground pepper

3 tablespoons finely chopped mixed herbs (parsley, chives, chervil, sweet basil, tarragon etc.)

6 tablespoons olive oil

❶ Remove the stalk from the lettuce, wash, trim and spin dry. Tear the leaves to a suitable size.

❷ Mix the vinegar with some salt and pepper and stir in the herbs. Whisk in the oil with a balloon whisk.

❸ Add the dressing and toss the salad just before serving.

Loin of veal

Preparation time: 2 hours

❶ Rub the meat all over with salt. Heat oil in a large pan and sear the meat thoroughly.

❷ Peel the onions and cut into large pieces. Add to the meat in the pan and cook briefly together. Pour in the white wine and add the spices. Pre-heat the oven to 250°C, 480°F, gas mark 9.

❸ Braise the veal in the pre-heated oven for about 15 minutes. Pour in 100 ml/3¼ fl oz (⅓ cup plus 1½ tablespoon) water, lower the heat to 200°C, 400°F, gas mark 6 and continue to cook for another 75 minutes. Remove from the oven and allow to rest for 10 minutes so that the roast does not lose any of its juices when being carved.

❹ Pour the roasting juices through a sieve (strainer), spoon in the crème fraîche and season with salt and pepper.

2 kg/4½ lbs loin of veal

salt

4 tablespoons oil

2 onions

250 ml/8½ fl oz (1 cup) white wine

6 sage leaves

1 sprig tarragon

150 g/5¼ oz crème fraîche

freshly ground pepper

Green beans with lemon sauce

Preparation time: 1 hour and 30 minutes

❶ Wash and top and tail (trim) the beans. Cook in boiling salted water for about 10 minutes until still crisp. Rinse at once in ice water and drain.

❷ Wash the lemons in hot water and rub dry. Peel paper-thin and cut into very fine strips (julienne). Blanch in a little boiling water for 2 minutes.

❸ Cut 3 thin slices of lemon and set aside. Squeeze the juice of the remaining lemons and – with salt and pepper, strips of lemon peel and olive oil – mix to make a dressing.

❹ Wash and trim the scallions and chop finely. Wash the parsley, pat dry and chop the leaves finely.

❺ Mix the dressing, the scallions and the parsley with the beans. Cut the lemon slices in half. Arrange the beans on 1–2 platters and garnish with the lemon slices.

1 kg/2¼ lbs green beans (or haricot beans)

salt

1½ unsprayed lemons

freshly ground pepper

10 tablespoons olive oil

2 scallions

1 large bunch smooth-leafed (flat) parsley

500 g/1 lb white bread

150 g5¼ oz onions

**50 g/1¾ oz (3½ tablespoons)
butter**

5 egg yolks

375 ml/12½ fl oz (1½ cups) milk

salt

freshly ground pepper

1 tablespoon chopped parsley

2 egg whites

8 tablespoons oil

Tea towel (dish towel) dumpling

Preparation time: 3 hours, 30 minutes

❶ Cut the crust off the bread and cut the bread into 1 cm/½ in large cubes. Put in a large bowl. Peel the onions and chop up small. Heat the butter in a frying pan and fry the onions. Spoon over the cubes of bread and mix in well.

❷ Beat the egg yolks with the milk and season with salt and pepper. Mix the egg and milk mixture and the chopped parsley with the bread. Cover and set aside to soak for about 2 hours.

❸ Beat the egg whites with a pinch of salt until they stand up in peaks and fold into the bread mixture.

❹ Scrape out the bread onto a clean tea towel (lay along the side of the tea towel, about 25 cm/10 in long). Roll up the tea towel and tie the ends tightly. Brush the cloth with oil on the outside

❺ Put the cloth in a large pot with boiling salted water and allow to steep – barely – simmering for about 1 hour.

❻ Take the dumpling out of the pot and allow to rest for a further 10 minutes. Remove the cloth carefully and cut the dumpling into slices.

Bavarian cream

Preparation time: 60 minutes, plus cooling time

❶ Soak 3 leaves of the gelatine in cold water. Pick over the berries, put in a pot with 100 g/3½ oz sugar, 1 sachet vanilla sugar, lemon juice and 3 tablespoons water and bring to the boil. Cover and simmer gently over a low heat for 5 minutes.

❷ Pass the berries through a sieve (strainer). Squeeze out the gelatine, add leaf by leaf to the hot fruit sauce and stir until it dissolves. Put the mixture somewhere cool.

❸ Soak the rest of the gelatine in cold water. Cut open the vanilla pod (bean) and scrape out the seeds. Pour the milk into a saucepan, add the pod and the seeds and bring slowly to the boil.

❹ Beat the egg yolks with the remaining sugar and vanilla sugar until they are creamy. While stirring constantly, pour in the hot – but not boiling – milk. Remove the vanilla pod (bean). Stir the mixture over a double boiler until it takes on a creamy consistency.

❺ Squeeze out the leaves of gelatine and stir one by one into the warm cream until they have dissolved. Pour the cream into a cold pan over a dish of ice cold water and beat until it starts to gel. Whip the single (whipping) cream and fold into the mixture.

❻ Set 2 tablespoons of the fruit mixture aside. Spoon the cream and the raspberry mixture into a glass bowl alternately. Decorate with the remaining raspberry mixture. Set aside to cool for at least 1 hour.

7 leaves white gelatine

450 g/1 lb raspberries (fresh or frozen)

185 g/6¼ oz sugar

2 sachets vanilla sugar

2 tablespoons lemon juice

1 vanilla pod (bean)

250 ml/8½ fl oz (1 cup) milk

4 egg yolks

250 ml/8½ fl oz (1 cup) single (whipping) cream

Checkliste

On the day before the party
☐ make the cinnamon croutons

☐ top and tail the beans, cook and rinse

☐ make the Bavarian cream (in the evening)

On the morning of the party
☐ prepare the lettuce, make vinaigrette

☐ finish making the beans in lemon sauce

3–4 hours before the guests arrive
☐ make the tea towel (dish towel) dumpling

☐ make the roast loin of veal

½–1 hour before the guests arrive
☐ make the Terlaner wine soup

☐ toss the lettuce with the vinaigrette

☐ prepare the apple and raspberry drink

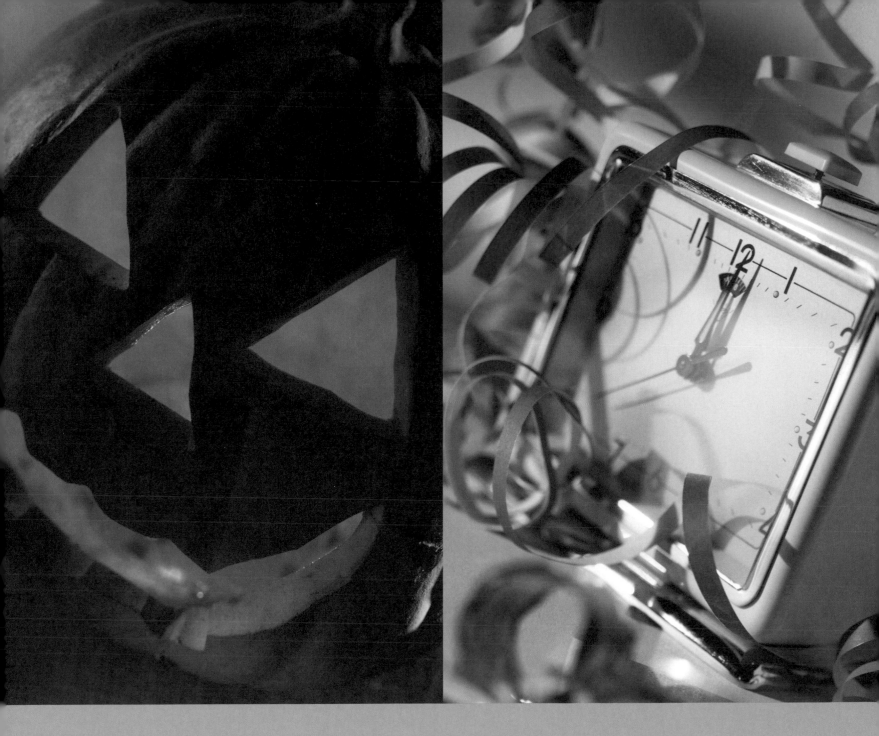

Parties for all seasons

Whether spring, summer, autumn or winter,
there is always a good reason for a party whatever the season.

The beginning of a new year:
New Year's Day party

Why not keep the momentum going from the party of the night before and continue the celebrations? After long and lavish partying on New Year's Eve, New Year's Day tends to be spent very quietly. This, however, does not mean that the party can not go on. In order to start the new year in good order after a wild party the night before, a leisurely and abundant New Year's brunch can help to revive depleted life forces.

Brunch is actually the gentle transition from breakfast to lunch, but in the case of a New Year's brunch, breakfast will probably be more welcome at lunchtime. Inviting people for 12 o'clock onwards will be fine. Sweets and hearty food, and cold and hot dishes will put life back into everybody. Apart from the usual delicacies to be found at a buffet brunch, emphasis should be put on the classical herring salad, and lots of vitamin C in the form of citrus fruits and orange juice.

TABLE AND BUFFET The new year is supposed to bring luck. Therefore lucky symbols should be the basis of the decorations. Cover the buffet with a dark tablecloth, black is best, or a large sheet which has been dyed. Paper streamers can tumble and coil across the table and little lucky figures of chimney sweeps, four-leaf clovers etc. made out of pipe cleaners can play hide and seek amongst them. Plant bushy green plants into little black pots, attach further lucky symbols such as little horse shoes, bright new pennies and so on to wires and stick them in the soil. You can also distribute fortune cookies with a lavish hand over the whole buffet.

THEME PARTY "In the secret service of my friends." The need for many, especially on a sunny New Year's morning, to hide their eyes behind dark glasses can be turned to advantage in a little game of fancy dress. The dress code can be dark suits and dark glasses à la the Blues Brothers. Darken the room in which you are having the party and use lights to illuminate certain areas.

Even the invitation can be a harbinger of mystery: write your lines with lemon juice on white paper. Only when the recipient heats the letter will he or she be able to read the text. (Don't forget to drop

a hint though!) Each guest will receive an alias in the same envelope. There is no limit to one's imagination in taking this game further.

The game of playing with identities can be extended as desired. If the invitation contains a new personality – sex, age, profession, hobbies and so on – then it can be a rule that the new "persona" be played for a certain time at some point during the party. This is a particularly attractive game if the guests are not well known to each other, but can even be full of surprises among old friends who suddenly find out new things about each other in this amusing way. As with most role-playing games, this game is also suitable for the New Year's Eve party or for any other celebration.

A celebration of lovers:
Valentine's Day

*Valentine of Ternin married a pair of lovers on February 14th , 269 in what was then –
under the Romans – still a forbidden Christian ritual. He was arrested and condemned
to death. Ever since, February 14th has been celebrated as the day of lovers. During the
Middle Ages it was mainly celebrated in Italy, France and England. Later it found
its way to the USA. Since the Second World War it has also become popular in German-
speaking countries.*

Today the noble rose is the symbol of love, but those who would like to revive a long-forgotten custom should choose the violet. Ever since Valentine's Day originated in the Middle Ages, it has been the little blue flower which has "spoken" for the shy young man, too timid to tell his love openly that he adores her. Another symbol of love is the heart, the characteristic shape of which, cut out of red, shiny card, makes a perfect dinner invitation.

DÉCOR Soft lighting, where possible only candle-light, is of course necessary for the desired atmosphere on this romantic day. One should, however, make sure there is enough light to eat by so that small accidents do not disturb the mood of the evening.

The centerpiece should be a heart of roses. For this you will need following materials:
• wire (2.5 m/8 ft long, 2 mm/0.8 in thick)
• thin wire (1 spool)
• moss (2 bags)
• green branches (ivy, box etc.)
• pliers with wire cutter
• roses, red and white

Cut the thicker wire into two pieces of the same length, each twice as high as the finished heart is to be. Join the two pieces in the middle and twist the ends together. Draw a heart of the desired size on a piece of cardboard. Lay the wire on this pattern and with the help of the pliers, bend it to the required shape. Attach the moss by binding it around the framework with the fine wire so that the thick wire can no longer be seen. Lay the green branches on this bed of moss and tie them on with the fine wire. Finally, cut off the heads of the roses leaving enough stalk to be able to wrap the fine wire around. Use the end of the wire to stick the roses on to the heart.

HINT If you would like to keep the heart to decorate your apartment for longer than a day or two, use silk roses or dried ones instead of fresh roses.

INVITATION CARDS Heart-shaped cards that open out are suitable for invitations. Here you will need some shiny red card, 28 x 12 cm/11 x 4.7 in. Enlarge the sketch below by 10 cm/4 in, copy onto paper and cut out. The sketch can now be used as a stencil for the red card. Draw around the hearts and then cut them out. Do not cut through the middle. Fold the card in the middle so that you get a single heart instead of two. Now you can write all the necessary information pertaining to your party – time, place, etc. – on the inside.

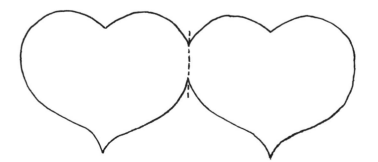

St. Valentine – the patron saint of lovers

For many centuries February 14th has had a special meaning for lovers, fiancées, good friends and relatives. On Valentine's day, named for St. Valentine, people like to show their affection for each other by means of small tokens, tender messages, gentle teasing, flowers, chocolates or small presents.

St. Valentine, a Christian martyr, lived in Rome in the year 269 and was reputedly put to death because he married a young couple using the Christian ritual. This is why he is seen today as the patron saint of lovers and as a marriage maker. He also happens to be the patron saint of bee-keepers. The date probably goes back to the feast of the goddess Juno, which the Romans used to celebrate on February 14th. On this day people did not just bring offerings of flowers to the goddess of the hearth and the family, but also to the women in one's own family. During the Middle Ages in the Hansa cities in Europe, a custom developed of having so-called "friendship dinners" at which sailors, merchants and craftsmen got together for a friendly meal. However, this day still remains the day of lovers.

When and where in Europe the superstition first arose that a young girl would marry the first man she saw on Valentine's day is hidden in the mists of time. However, it has been the custom in many parts of Europe, at least since the Middle Ages, that on February 14th early in the morning young men are to be found standing outside the houses of their loved ones with large bunches of flowers in order to ensure their being the lucky one. In the ecclesiastical year, liturgies are sung around February 14th with the theme "arrival of the groom." In France the 14th was seen as the day of the bridal couple. A young man too shy to tell his beloved that he adored her could give her a flower on Valentine's day – usually a violet or a bunch of violets – and be understood without saying a word.

There is also a further, much more prosaic explanation for the giving of flowers on this day: the middle of February was traditionally a day called "much love day." This was the day that farmers and gardeners used to pick a certain kind of lettuce which had survived the winter under the snow cover, a lettuce called "much love"... In England and Scotland, where Valentine's Day has a long tradition, the following game was played by young people on the day of the Roman saint: the names of all the young unmarried girls were written on little pieces of paper and thrown into a pot. The young men would then pull one out without looking and were pledged to show many little courtesies and
attentions over the year to the girl whose name they had drawn. No wonder that many marriages resulted from this!

Up until the end of the second World War, Valentine's Day was celebrated mainly in Britain, in France and in the USA. Now lovers all over the world send each other greetings, presents and flowers on Saint Valentine's Day, on February 14th.

Menu

White lady

Fig and ham hors-d'oeuvre

Tomato consommé with shrimps

Cod fillet in tomato and tarragon
sauce with peas

Saddle of venison with chanterelle
and juniper cream sauce

Espresso cream
with Amaretto mandarin oranges

Serves
4 people

Per glass

2 egg whites

sugar

ice

30 ml/1 fl oz (2 tablespoons) gin

15 ml/½ fl oz (1 tablespoon) Cointreau

15 ml/½ fl oz (1 tablespoon) lemon juice

White lady

Preparation time: 4 minutes

❶ Tip the egg whites onto a flat plate, beat well and dip the rim of the champagne glass in them. Then dip the glass into a bowl of sugar and turn several times so that the sugar sticks evenly to the rim of the glass.

❷ Put the ice, gin, Cointreau and the lemon juice into the shaker with a little bit of the egg white and shake well.

❸ Pour through a barkeeper's sieve (strainer) into the prepared champagne glasses.

Fig and ham hors-d'oeuvre

Preparation time: 5 minutes

❶ Wash the figs, pat dry, and cut in half. Arrange a piece of ham on each of the fig halves and use a cocktail stick or toothpick to hold it.

2 fresh blue figs
4 very thin slices of Parma ham

Tomato consommé with shrimps

Preparation time: 2 hours and 30 minutes

❶ Trim the leek, wash and cut into pieces. Peel the garlic. Wash the tomatoes, cut in half and remove the stalk ends.

❷ Heat the butter in a soup pot and brown the marrow bones together with the leek and the garlic. Add the tomatoes and fill up the pot with 2 liters/3½ pints of water. Simmer over a low heat for about 2 hours. Pour through a sieve (strainer) and allow to cool.

❸ Clarify the bouillon with the egg white and add salt, pepper and sugar to taste.

❹ Put four shrimps in each plate and pour the hot soup over them.

½ leek
1 clove of garlic
500 g/1¼ lbs tomatoes
1 tablespoon butter
2 marrow bones
1 egg white
salt
freshly ground pepper
1 pinch sugar
16 shrimps

HINT How to clarify consommé:
Beat the egg white until it forms peaks. Add a little of the bouillon and put the mixture in a pot. Add the rest of the bouillon to the egg whites while stirring constantly and bring to the boil. Remove from heat and drain through a cheesecloth.

Cod fillet in tomato and tarragon sauce with peas

600 g/1¼ lb cod fillets

herb salt

freshly ground pepper

4 small tomatoes

1 large shallot

15 g/1 oz (1 tablespoon) butter

1 small bunch dill, chopped

100 ml/4 fl oz (½ cup) dry white wine

200 ml/8 fl oz (½ cup) tomato sauce (see page 126, or use a commercial product)

1 small bunch tarragon, finely chopped

15 g/1 oz (1 tablespoon) chilled butter pieces

500 g/18 oz peas

salt

❶ Set the oven to a very low heat, 80°C/175°F. Rinse the cod fillet, wipe dry and cut into portion-size pieces. Season with herb salt and pepper. Cut the tomatoes into quarters, remove the seeds and cut into strips. Peel the shallots and chop finely.

❷ Butter a saucepan. Add the dill, shallot and white wine. Add the fish. Cover and steam gently over a low heat until cooked. Keep warm in the oven.

❸ Strain the fish juices through a fine sieve and pour into a small saucepan. Boil the liquid down almost completely. Add the tomato sauce and bring to the boil. Stir in the tomato strips and tarragon. Season with herb salt and pepper. Add the pieces of butter, one at a time.

❹ Cook the peas in salted water and drain.

❺ Pour the tomato sauce onto four warmed plates and arrange the fish and peas on top.

Spring is in the air
Easter

As is the case with Christmas Day, Easter is also a day when the family meets and celebrates together. However, Easter is not just a Christian or pagan festival, it is also the time of year in which Nature awakes from her long winter sleep and the days become warmer. The gentle twittering of birds and the blossoming of buds and flowers are unmistakable signs of the end of the cold and the beginning of spring.

The early afternoon, after lunch, is probably the best time for a traditional German Easter game – the Easter rabbit game – in which all can join in. One or two players are chosen as hunters, the others are all rabbits with a handkerchief hanging out of their back pockets to mark them as such. The hunters have to catch as many rabbits as possible, the winner is whoever is the last to remain free.

DECORATIONS The main decorations for the festive buffet are Easter nests made of yeast dough and filled with delicately colored eggs. Tulips made of wood are also an attractive accent. For 10 tulips you will need the following:
• 1 piece of plywood, 60 cm/24 in square, 3 mm/⅛ in thick
• tracing paper and carbon paper
• rough and fine sandpaper
• yellow, white and green paint
• clear varnish

First of all the patterns must be copied onto the tracing paper. Then the copies are transferred to the wood and sawn out carefully. Sand any rough edges with the sandpaper. Now paint the stalks green and the blossoms yellow. Highlight effects can be painted on with the white paint. Once the paint has dried the flowers can be varnished.

INVITATIONS Here one can carry on the theme of the table decorations: draw a flower on pale yellow paper, cut the flower shape out, and write your invitation on it.

A Christian festival with pagan roots

Easter, a significant Christian festival, is at the same time the one richest in pagan symbolism. Easter egg, Easter rabbit and even the name are all relics of the old Germanic-Celtic spring rites. Whereas the name in the south European and Latin countries stems from the Jewish Passover, in Germany and Britain it probably comes from the Germanic goddess of spring, Ostara. The name of the point of the compass "east" comes from the Indo-Germanic word "audes", meaning the rose-colored dawn. In regional customs one finds many old rites. In some places, on Easter night, girls go at midnight to fetch water from a certain spring. Legend has it that if it is brought home in silence, then it will help heal all kinds of sickness. In other places, the young men are allowed to beat the young girls with artistically decorated palm branches, this is said to bestow fertility. In yet other places, a straw doll is burned in the Easter bonfire. This was originally meant to represent the dying of winter, but was later reinterpreted to signify the biblical Judas.

The egg is a symbol of new life in nearly all cultures. In the Middle Ages it was a form of tribute to the feudal lord, but also a valuable gift, for instance to one's beloved. Later, among the aristocracy, a custom arose in which they gave each other decorated golden eggs. In the USA and England, the children hide nests they have made themselves before Easter and hope that they will find them filled the next morning. Hunting for Easter eggs is also well-known in Germany. There are also many other competitions involving Easter eggs. In England, each

Kiwi cocktail

Preparation time: 10 minutes

2 kiwis

2 tablespoons lime juice

2 tablespoons woodruff syrup

700 ml/24 fl oz (3 cups) dry champagne or sparkling wine (ice cold)

❶ Peel the kiwis, purée with the lime juice and the woodruff syrup.

❷ Pour the kiwi syrup into the glasses and fill with the ice-cold sparkling wine. Serve immediately.

Asparagus platter

Preparation time: 1 hour and 15 minutes

1½ kg/2¼ lbs green asparagus

2 kg/2½ lbs white asparagus

2 liters/3½ pints (8cups) vegetable stock

50 g/1¾ oz (3½ tablespoons) butter

salt

5 tablespoons sugar

❶ Peel the asparagus, remove the woody ends and bind together in portions with kitchen thread.

❷ Bring the stock to the boil with the butter, salt and sugar. Lay the asparagus in the pot, cover and cook for 15–20 minutes. Remove from the water and allow to drain. Arrange on a platter, serve with hollandaise sauce.

Hollandaise sauce

Preparation time: 20 minutes

500 g/1 lb (2 cups) melted butter

6 egg yolks

2 teaspoons salt

½ teaspoon freshly ground pepper

2 tablespoons lemon juice

❶ Heat the butter, skim and allow to cool.

❷ Whisk the egg yolks in a bowl and add 2 tablespoons of water, salt, pepper and the lemon juice. Place over a double boiler.

❸ Beat the egg mixture until it is very light and frothy.

❹ Add the clarified butter carefully, continually whisking until you have a creamy sauce.

The winter is really on its way out
The spring party

When the last traces of snow have melted and the days are getting longer, Nature starts to wake up from her long winter's sleep. The first buds and blossoms peek out every-where. Amongst all this fresh green is a very special plant – the woodruff. It is sought after in order to make that traditional harbinger of spring, May punch. This mixture of fresh herbs, wine and champagne makes a refreshing and popular drink.

May punch is a special variation among the myriad of ways of making punch. Woodruff is freshly available only for a couple of weeks in the year and it is this that gives the punch its unique and delicious taste. The joyous elation that arises from springtime and punch should be reflected in the décor of the venue for the party.

DECORATION White tablecloths are the basis of the buffet, but the mood is set by adding linden green and pale lilac cloths that include accents of darker lilac which are reminiscent of violets and crocuses. Draped generously in flowing forms, these pastel colored cloths cover the white tablecloths with the cloth in the main color predominating. The flowers carry the emphasis on the color lilac further. Different spring flowers, all in bloom, either from bulbs in pots or freshly cut, such as violets, forget-me-nots, crocuses and primroses arranged here and there create a delightful springtime atmosphere.

INVITATION CARDS A recurring motif running through the whole party can be an invitation in the shape of a flower that you make yourself. The amount of paper you will need will depend on the number of guests. You will need the following:
• white card
• dark lilac construction paper
• black construction paper

First of all you need a stencil to draw around so that all the invitations are the same shape. Start by drawing a flower shape on the white card. It should be big enough so that there is room to write the invitation in the middle. It is best to start with an oval shape which is the middle of the flower. You need two of these, one

of which has the flower shape drawn around it. Now you can cut out the stencil, lay it on the colored paper and draw around it. This is then also cut out. Now make a further oval stencil for the black paper. The black oval shapes are the center of the flower. You can draw around the flower with a black pen in order to bring out the contours better and then all you have to do is to write your invitation inside the flower.

Dear Helen and Andrew,
You are cordially
invited by
The Easter Rabbit
to a festive meal
on the 23 April at 12:30.

Please let us know
by next week
if you will be able to
come or not.

Strawberry punch

Preparation time: 20 minutes, plus time for marinating

700 g/25 oz strawberries

125 ml/4 fl oz (½ cup) white rum

700 ml/24 fl oz (3 cups) dry white
   wine (chilled)

500 ml/17 fl oz (2 cups) orange juice

2 tablespoons lemon juice

fresh mint leaves to garnish

1.4 liters/48 fl oz (6 cups) dry champagne or sparkling wine (chilled)

❶ Wash the strawberries, trim and cut into slices.

❷ Mix the fruit with the rum, white wine, orange and lemon juice and allow to steep for about 4 hours.

❸ Wash the mint leaves and pat dry. Pour the chilled champagne into the punch just before serving. Decorate with the mint leaves.

Kiwi punch

Preparation time: 20 minutes, plus time for marinating

5–6 kiwis

1 tablespoon lemon juice

1 tablespoon white rum

2 tablespoons cognac

250 ml/ dry white wine

700 ml/24 fl oz (3 cups) dry champagne or sparkling wine (chilled)

1 star fruit to garnish

❶ Peel the kiwis carefully with a potato peeler and cut into slices.

❷ Mix the fruit with lemon juice, rum, cognac and wine. Allow to steep for at least 2 hours.

❸ Pour the champagne into the punch just before serving. Wash the star fruit, cut into slices and decorate the punch with them.

Crostini with oil and tomatoes

Preparation time: 20 minutes

5 beef tomatoes

10 slices crusty white bread
   (1 cm/½ in thick)

3 cloves of garlic

olive oil

salt

❶ Pour boiling water over the tomatoes, peel and cut off the stalk ends. Cut into small dice.

❷ Toast the slices of bread and cut in half.

❸ Peel the garlic and cut in half. Rub it over the pieces of toast then drizzle olive oil over them.

❹ Arrange the diced tomato on the pieces of toast and season with salt.

Eating out of doors
The picnic

The word "picnic" means "to pick up something small" and was, at the time the word was coined, quite a decadent junket. In the days – in the 18th and 19th centuries – when it was all the rage among the aristocracy and the rich to go out to the country and lose some of their fashionable pallor, the "something small" was a roast pheasant, venison or wild boar. Today, as there are no more servants to carry the roast game, things are a bit more simple, but the main thing is that they are fun.

All occasions and reasons are ideal for having a picnic. Eating out of doors can be made very comfortable with an arbour and a couple of picnic tables. If you don't have the necessary equipment at home, it is easy to rent or else very cheap to buy in a DIY shop.
Planning a picnic takes some care, as what doesn't go into the basket when it is being packed will be missing at the party later. Here is a list of the basic necessities:
• enough plates
• enough glasses or beakers (cups)
• enough cutlery (flatware)
• one or two sharp knives
• several bottle openers
• several corks or lids
• lots of napkins
• tea towels (dish towels)
• tablecloths

If the summer party in the country is meant to turn into an idyllic summer night's party, then lighting needs to be thought of even though the days are longer in the summer. Colored lanterns or garden torches made of wax will make the Arabian-British

Coffee with cognac

Put 1 teaspoon sugar in a cup and fill up with hot coffee. Add 2 cl/¾ fl oz (1 tablespoon and 1 teaspoon) cognac and a dash of orange bitters.

Coffee with almond liqueur

Put a teaspoon of brown sugar in a cup and fill up with hot coffee. Add 2 cl/¾ fl oz (1 tablespoon and 1 teaspoon) of Amaretto, put a little bitter almond biscuit on the spoon and serve.

Coffee with orange liqueur

Sprinkle a teaspoon of vanilla sugar into a cup and fill up with hot coffee. Add 2 cl/¾ fl oz (1 tablespoon and 1 teaspoon) of Grand Marnier and decorate with whipped cream.

HINT Make the coffee in advance at home and take it with you in thermos flasks. Don't forget the sugar, brown sugar and vanilla sugar nor the cognac, orange bitters, Amaretto, Grand-Marnier and the little amarettini and the whipped cream. It would be advisable to decant the alcohol into small bottles to take with you.

Mushroom salad

Preparation time: 20 minutes

❶ Wipe the mushrooms with kitchen paper (paper towels), cut the big mushrooms into quarters or halves and sprinkle with lemon juice.

❷ Pour boiling water over the tomatoes, peel, cut off the stalk ends and chop into small pieces. Peel the shallots and cut in half.

❸ Heat the oil in a pot and fry the shallots while stirring. Add the mushrooms and fry briefly. Stir in the tomatoes and the white wine. Season with the peppercorns, salt, cloves and cinnamon. Cover and simmer gently for about 15 minutes.

❹ Put the mushrooms into a bowl or onto a platter and allow to cool. Wash the parsley, pat dry, remove the stalks and chop finely. Sprinkle over the mushrooms.

1 kg/2½ lbs firm mushrooms

2 tablespoons lemon juice

4 tomatoes

15 shallots

5 tablespoons olive oil

500 ml/17 fl oz (2 cups) dry white wine

2 tablespoons pickled green peppercorns
herb salt

1 pinch ground cloves

1 pinch cinnamon powder

1 bunch parsley

Hot parties in the cool shade
Summer parties

Partying in the fresh air under blue summer skies is still one of the nicest ways to celebrate. For a summer party, deciding who to invite can be fairly easy, and if you are going to have a barbecue the preparations are also fairly simple. Sauces, dressings and dips can all be made in advance, the beer comes in a barrel and a couple of bottles of country wine are easy to find. The only thing that you have no control over is the weather.

Another problem could be deciding where to have it, as, after a fairly short time, peole may be able to neither hear nor smell anything else. Those who have a garden might be well-advized to invite the neighbors, as the smell of charcoal and sizzling sausages has upset more than one neighborhood friendship.

Trestle or picnic tables prove themselves to be useful articles of furniture in the garden or in a park. They are fairly cheap to buy during the summer months in DIY markets, but if you do not celebrate often out of doors, it might be more economical to rent tables and benches at a liquor store or party service. Don't forget to think about lighting, even if it stays lighter longer in the summer months.

DRINKS

The most suitable drink is beer. Shandy is also a good idea (500 ml/17 fl oz (2 cups) lager mixed with 500 ml/17 fl oz (2 cups) lemonade. However, you should always have a sufficient amount of non-alcoholic drinks on hand such as fruit juices for children or alcohol-free beer for those wanting to drive.

So that the preparations do not take up too much time, the recipes for the barbecue should be varied

but also uncomplicated. This is why we suggest various marinades for meat, fish, poultry and lamb. To round off the selection, you can offer grilled potatoes, various salads and spiced butter.

PREPARATION

Before the barbecue starts and the first guests arrive, you should check that you have everything necessary:

• long-handled tongs and forks
• a bellows for the charcoal
• lighter fuel or starter briquettes
• sufficient charcoal
• barbecue gloves (optional)

HINT The warmer the summer night, the greater the danger of thunderstorms. A far-sighted host who does not own a garden house will set up a tent or tarpaulin before the party begins where guests can find refuge should there be rain showers. Because of the danger of poisoning from the smoke, however, the barbecue should be set up under another roof. Public barbecue spots often have a small roofed area or something similar where one can escape from the rain.

Barbeque sauces

Peanut sauce
Preparation time: 12 minutes

Grind the peanuts very finely in a food blender. Cut the chili peppers length-ways, remove seeds and chop finely. Blend both chills and peanuts together with the rest of the ingredients in the blender.

120 g/4oz peanuts

2 red chili peppers

2 teaspoons curry powder

1 teaspoon turmeric

250 ml/8½ fl oz (1 cup) single (whipping) cream

2 tablespoons soy sauce

2 tablespoons lemon juice

Yoghurt sauce with curry
Preparation time: 15 minutes

❶ Fry the pine kernels briefly in a pan without oil. Peel the onions, cut into small dice. Add the oil to the pine kernels, heat, and fry the onions. Sprinkle on the curry powder and cook for a short time.

❷ Add the pine kernel mixture to the yoghurt. Season with salt and pepper. Wash the chives, snip finely and stir in.

20 g/¾ oz pine kernels

2 onions

2 tablespoons olive oil

1 tablespoon curry powder

300 ml/10 fl oz (1¼ cup) cream yoghurt

salt

freshly ground pepper

1 bunch chives

Herb sauce
Preparation time: 10 minutes

❶ Stir the mustard, yoghurt and lemon juice together to make a smooth sauce. Season with salt and pepper and add the herbs.

❷ Whip the cream until thick and stir into the herb sauce.

1 teaspoon mustard

125 g/4½ oz low fat milk yoghurt

1 tablespoon lemon juice

salt

freshly ground pepper

2 tablespoons chopped herbs: parsley, chives, chervil, dill, green coriander (cilantro)

100 ml/3½ oz (scant ½ cup) cream

The autumn festival
Halloween

There are plenty of reasons for having parties in the autumn: Harvest Home, wine festivals and church feast days are some of the classical ones in Europe that are celebrated with young wine of the region and other delicacies. Halloween is also becoming more popular. This is a festival in which the pumpkin plays a large role, not just as a sweet and sour relish beloved by many, but as a decoration and symbol that is thought to drive away witches and ghosts afraid of the light.

Halloween as it is celebrated today is one of the youngest imports of the American way of life to Europe. It is a mixture of Harvest Home and carnival. Children like to frighten the grown-ups and each other, and to roam through the streets dressed up in scary costumes and demanding sweets. The adults also like to get together on Halloween, and get dressed up as spooky figures too. The overriding symbol of this activity is the pumpkin, which, along with various other eerie decorations, is the main theme of the party.

DECORATIONS

A large white cloth is decorated with autumnal leaf motifs for the tablecloth. Apart from using potato stamps, you can cut stencils out of card and, after drawing around them, the patterns can be painted with all the golden colors of autumn. Vine leaves can be scattered over the table. Small decorative pumpkins, as well as the large ones can be used. For a candlestick, cut a lid off a small pumpkin and hollow out enough room for a candle. Make sure that the candle doesn't wobble.

A hollowed-out pumpkin with a grinning face is of course a necessity for a Halloween party. The pumpkin left over from making the delicious pumpkin dishes will do perfectly for a large, glowing face. First of all cut a lid off with a sharp knife. If you hold the knife at a slant you will have a smooth edge. Now remove the flesh with a big spoon. You might need a sturdy knife as you get closer to the rind. Draw the face on the pumpkin rind before cutting out the eyes, nose and mouth. Use a very sharp knife and cut along the contours you have drawn. Put a short candle or a nightlight inside, light it and put the lid back on. There is no limit to your imagination, the main thing being: the spookier the better.

INVITATIONS

For the invitations, start by drawing a pumpkin face on paper. Cut this out and use it as a stencil. Lay the stencil on colored paper, draw around it and then cut out the pumpkin invitation. Write in the time and place.

Pot-roast with mushrooms

Preparation time: 4 hours

1 kg/21/4 lbs mushrooms

1 bunch scallions

1 bunch celery sticks

1½ kg/3¼ lbs brisket

salt

freshly ground pepper

125 ml/4 fl oz (½ cup) oil

2 tablespoons dried thyme

1 tablespoon chopped rosemary

1 tablespoon chopped tarragon

1 tablespoon chopped marjoram

500 ml/17 fl oz (2 cups) white wine

2 tablespoons tomato purée (paste)

150 ml/5 fl oz (⅔ cup) crème fraîche

2 tablespoons gravy thickener (dark)

❶ Wipe the mushrooms with kitchen paper (paper towels) and cut in half. Trim and wash the scallions and cut into rings. Wash the celery and cut into slices.

❷ Cut the fat off the meat, rub in salt and pepper. Heat the oil and sear the meat on all sides. Transfer to a plate. Pre-heat the oven to 120°C, 225°F, gas mark 1.

❸ Next lightly brown the vegetables in the meat fat. When they are browned, move the vegetables to the side of the pan and put the meat back in the middle. Add the herbs and pour in the wine. Cover and leave in the oven for about 31/2 hours.

❹ Take the meat and vegetables out of the pan and put in a warm place. Stir the tomato purée (paste) and crème fraîche into the meat juices, boil briskly for ten minutes until reduced. Stir in the thickener and bring to the boil again. Season with salt and pepper.

❺ Cut the meat into slices, arrange on a platter with the vegetables. Serve with the gravy.

HINT The pot-roast only needs a good 30 minutes preparation, the rest of the time it roasts away in the oven without needing attention. Be careful to plan on the oven being free for this length of time!

A time for reflection
Christmas

There are many different ways of celebrating Christmas that have developed over the last 150 years. In Germany, for instance, the family stays at home on Christmas Eve and the other two days are full of visiting and receiving guests. Whatever the custom, whether one is celebrating an old-fashioned family Christmas at home, holding a ceremonial banquet or living it up at an "X-mas" party, the planning should ensure that the host or hostess can enjoy the festivities without undue stress.

The nice thing about Christmas is the length of time one has to look forward to it. At the beginning of December one can already find gingerbread and chocolate Santa Clauses in the supermarkets. In parts of Europe, the baking of Christmas cookies starts around this time. However, things tend to get stressful on Christmas Eve in the countries where the presents are opened on this day. Dinner has to be got ready, the presents wrapped, and still it is supposed to be a relaxed and reflective evening. The solution to this problem lies in careful planning. Choose meals that are easy to cook in advance and that can be frozen. Then you only have to thaw the food on the day of the feast and heat it up again.

DECORATIONS The color combination of dark blue and gold goes best with the festive character of Christmas. A white damask tablecloth decorated with gold and blue table runners will look wonderful. Set the table with large golden plates and white china place settings over these. Lay a rolled-up linen napkin on each plate. The bottom is tied with a lavish golden bow which might hold the place card also. A few slices of dried oranges, lemons, kiwis or other decorative dried fruits peek from the other end.

In the middle of the table, aromatic, spiced citrus fruits tied with blue and golden ribbons lie on a large fruit plate which is decorated with pine cones, moss and ivy leaves. The oranges, lemons and limes have had patterns engraved in their skins with a sharp knife. There are a myriad patterns to choose from: zigzags, spirals and many others. The fruits are then spiked with cloves and the blue and gold ribbons add the finishing touch.

Waiting for Father Christmas

The British attribute their version of Christmas to a tradition established by King Arthur. He is supposed to have celebrated Christ's birth with "harpists, flautists, jugglers and dancers" in a most jovial manner in York in 531. Music still plays a very important role in a British Christmas. Jingling bells, church bells and choir music provide the right Christmas atmosphere. In Wales local choirs in the villages compete to compose a new Christmas carol which is then sung by everybody the next year.

But the British do not celebrate advent, as the Germans do. Preparations for Christmas in Britain begin in late autumn and become more intense, the nearer it gets to the end of December. The Christmas cake and Christmas pudding are prepared in October so that they will be at their best for the festival. People buy a Christmas tree in mid-December and decorate it. And they dare not forget the mistletoe which is hung up over a door. Anybody can kiss anybody else under this. Special services take place in churches on Christmas Eve and Christmas Day. Children hang up their Christmas stockings when they go to bed on Christmas Eve and Father Christmas hopefully fills it during the night. Most children cannot wait to open their stockings very early in the morning – and their larger presents which are under the tree. The main festivities take place on December 25: presents are opened and families eat Christmas dinner together. People traditionally eat their Christmas turkey at lunch-time, followed by Christmas pudding.

Christmas celebrations were banned in the USA for years because the Puritans urged people to mark the occasion soberly. But the Americans finally took over the European tradition in the

Duck terrine

Preparation time: 3 hours, plus time for cooling

❶ Knead the flour, butter and one teaspoon salt together with 150 ml/5 fl oz (2/3 cup) ice-cold water. Cover and put somewhere cold for at least two hours. Line a baking tin (pan) (about 25 cm/10 in long) with greaseproof (waxed) paper.

❷ Wash the duck breast, pat dry, remove the fatty edges and brown on both sides in hot oil about one minute each side. Take out of the pan and allow to cool.

❸ Mix the minced meat with the crème fraîche, lemon peel, gingerbread spices and mustard. Season generously with salt and pepper.

❹ Roll out two thirds of the cooled pastry so that the edges extend beyond the tin (pan) and lift into the tin (pan). Spoon in half of the minced (ground) meat. Lay the duck's breast on top of this and cover with the remaining meat. Lift the edges of the pastry over the top and roll out the rest of the pastry to make a lid. With a pastry cutter, cut a round hole in the lid before covering the terrine. Cut decorations with a Christmas motif out of the rest of the pastry and decorate the crust with them. Pre-heat the oven to 180°C, 350°F, gas mark 4.

❺ Brush the crust with beaten egg and bake in the oven for about 90 minutes. Remove from the oven and pour off the liquid. Take carefully out of the tin (pan), allow to cool somewhat then return to the tin (pan) and allow to cool completely.

❻ Soak the gelatine in cold water. Take it out and squeeze. Heat the game broth and dissolve the gelatine leaf by leaf. Stir in the Marsala and season with salt and pepper. As soon as the liquid starts to gel, pour into the opening in the crust. Put in a cool place and allow to set.

❼ Take the terrine out of the tin (pan) and cut into thin slices.

500 g/1 lb plain (all-purpose) flour

250 g/½ lb (1 cup) butter

salt

350 g/12 oz duck breast

1 tablespoon oil

1 kg/2¼ lb minced (ground) pork

200 ml/7 fl oz (¾ cup) crème fraîche

1 sachet lemon peel

1 teaspoon mixed gingerbread spices

2 teaspoons mustard

freshly ground pepper

1 egg yolk

6 leaves white gelatine

400 ml/13½ fl oz (1⅗ cup) game broth (in a jar)

3 tablespoons Marsala (Italian dessert wine)

Saying goodbye to the old year
New Year's Eve party

The many variations of partying into the new year are unlimited: just the two of you at home, a visit to the theater, at the ski resort with midnight skiing by torchlight, at a five-star hotel with dinner, dancing and fireworks or as a host at your own party. Whatever the method, ushering in the new year is a cheerful occasion full of optimism at a time when you should surround yourself with people you like and who will contribute to the atmosphere of your party in a nice way.

On the longest night of the year one does not have to invite people for the usual time of seven or eight o'clock. Ten o'clock in the evening is a perfectly suitable time. However, you might then have to count on your guests already having had "one for the road" at their home or at another party. It is definitely a night for flexibility, as many people tend to go party-hopping and show up at various places trailing friends in their wake. This means that it is quite possible that hosts and hostess could find themselves entertaining people whom they do not even know. If all goes well, this is an added bonus for the party and its guests.

INVITATIONS The invitation can be a small surprise parcel in itself. Write the invitation on sliver paper and put it into an envelope with some confetti, a small Christmas cracker, a sparkler and various little figures that symbolize good luck for the coming year.

DECORATION The colors for a New Year's Eve buffet are a cool and futuristic silver look and a profound and romantic deep blue. For a round,

three-tiered buffet with a diameter of 150 cm/60 in you will need the following:

- 3 round plywood tabletops of 150 cm/60 in, 70 cm/28 in and 30 cm/12 in diameter, 30 mm/1¼ in thick
- 2 trestles
- 1 wooden crate
- 1 10-liter/2 gallons bucket
- flower pot or champagne bucket
- silver-grey tablecloths
- dark blue tablecloths

Lay the largest of the tabletops over the two trestles. Drape completely with dark blue cloth. On top of this comes the crate which should be covered with the silver-grey cloth. Mount the medium-sized table on top of the crate and cover with blue cloth. The bucket which has been wrapped in silver paper and turned upside-down is the support for the next tier. Place a silver flower pot or the champagne bucket on top of this and fill with ferns that have been sprayed silver. To these you can also add the year, cut out of silver cardboard.

Cream cheese fritters

Preparation time: 30 minutes

1 kg/2¼ lbs cream cheese

8 eggs

zest from 1 unsprayed lemon

freshly grated nutmeg

50 g/1¾ oz flour

olive oil for deep-frying

❶ Mix the cream cheese together with the eggs, lemon peel, 1 pinch nutmeg and the sifted flour.

❷ Heat enough oil in a deep pot or chip pan to 180°C, 350°F.

❸ Make balls from the cheese mixture of about 3–4 cm/1¼–1½ in diameter and fry in batches until golden yellow. Drain on crumpled kitchen paper (paper towels).

Veal with tuna sauce

Preparation time: 2 hours

1 onion

1 large carrot

2 sticks celery

500 ml/17 fl oz (2 cups) dry white
  wine

1 sprig rosemary

2 bay leaves

salt

1 kg/2¼ lbs lean veal

3 fresh egg yolks

200 ml/7 fl oz (¾ cup) olive oil

3–4 tablespoons lemon juice

1 tablespoon capers

4 anchovies

1 tin (can) tuna in oil (about
  300 g/10½ oz net weight)

freshly ground pepper

❶ Peel the onion and carrot and chop coarsely. Trim the celery, wash and cut into large pieces. Put the vegetables in a pot with the white wine, 500 ml/17 fl oz (2 cups) water, the sprig of rosemary, bay leaf and salt and bring to the boil. Wrap the meat in a cotton cloth, tie with kitchen string and put into the boiling broth. Simmer over a low heat for about 1½ hours until done. Do not allow to boil!

❷ Allow the meat to cool in the broth. While it is cooling beat the eggs and gradually add 100 ml/3½ fl oz (½ cup) of the oil in a thin stream while using the electric beater. You should have a creamy mayonnaise. Season with lemon juice and salt.

❸ Purée the capers, anchovies and drained tuna in a blender. Slowly add the remaining oil. Press the mixture through a sieve (strainer) and mix with the mayonnaise. Season with salt and pepper.

❹ Take the meat out of the broth, unwrap and cut into very thin slices. Spread some of the sauce on a platter, arrange the slices of meat on top and cover with the remaining sauce.

HINT Don't forget to serve several baskets of bread: crusty baguette cut diagonally and Italian white bread with herbs.

Zuppa Inglese

Preparation time: 1 hour and 30 minutes

250 ml/8½ fl oz (1 cup) milk

175 g/6 oz sugar

2 sachets vanilla sugar

2 vanilla pods (beans)

4 eggs

100 g/3½ oz powdered sugar

1 kg/2¼ lbs curd or cream cheese

100 g/3½ oz grated plain (dark) chocolate

50 ml/2 fl oz (3½ tablespoons) Amaretto

2 ready-made sponge cakes or a packet of sponge fingers

125 ml/4¼ oz (½ cup) rum

❶ In a saucepan, slowly heat the milk, 100 g/3½ oz sugar and the vanilla sugar. Do not allow to boil. Cut open the vanilla pods (beans) lengthways, scrape out the seeds and add them to the milk with the pods (beans). Allow to barely simmer over a low heat for 10 minutes then allow to cool. Remove the vanilla pods (beans).

❷ Cream 2 eggs, 1 egg yolk and 100 g/3½ oz powdered sugar until foamy. Slowly stir in the cooled milk.

❸ Press the curd or cream cheese through a sieve (strainer), mix with the egg and milk mixture, the chocolate and 20 ml/¾ fl oz (1½ tablespoons) Amaretto.

❹ Cut the sponge into 4 cm/1½ in wide pieces and lay one third of the pieces in an ovenproof dish. Pour over 40 ml/2½ (tablespoons) rum and one third of the cream. Continue adding the rest of the ingredients in the same order. Allow the dessert to stand for at least 2 hours in a cool place. Pre-heat the oven to 240°C, 475°F, gas mark 9.

❺ Beat two egg whites until they stand up in peaks, put in a piping bag and decorate the Zuppa Inglese. Bake briefly in the pre-heated oven until the tips of the meringue turn golden brown.

> **HINT** In the original Italian recipe, the Zuppa Inglese is made with ricotta (soft Italian cheese) instead of curds. It is available in the better supermarkets.

Midnight soup

Preparation time: 45 minutes

6 large onions

2 leeks

2 red bell peppers

2 yellow bell peppers

2 green bell peppers

2 tins (cans) kidney beans

500 g/1 lb minced (ground) meat

5 tablespoons olive oil

2 liters/3½ pints (8 cups) instant meat
    stock

500 ml/17 fl oz (2 cups) dry red wine

salt

sugar

paprika powder

chili powder

❶ Peel the onions and chop finely. Trim the leeks, wash thoroughly and cut into fine rings. Remove the seeds from the bell peppers, wash and cut into thin strips. Drain the beans in a sieve (strainer).

❷ Brown the minced (ground) meat over a high heat in hot oil. Add the onions, leeks and bell peppers and stew for about 10 minutes. Add the beans, pour in the stock, cover and cook for another 15 minutes.

❸ Add the red wine and give the soup a fiery flavor with salt, sugar, paprika and chili powder.

Checklist

On the day before the party

☐ prepare the cauliflower and broccoli quiche

☐ cook the midnight soup

☐ prepare the veal with tuna sauce (steps 1–3)

☐ prepare the Zuppa Iglese (steps 1–4)

On the morning of the party

☐ make the potato salad

☐ prepare the cream cheese fritters (step 1)

3–4 hours before the guests arrive

☐ prepare the smoked salmon salad

½–1 hour before the guests arrive

☐ finish the veal and tuna sauce (step 4)

☐ deep-fry the cream cheese fritters (steps 2–3)

Just before the guests arrive

☐ finish the smoked salmon salad

☐ quickly brown the Zuppa Inglese in the oven (step 5)

Theme parties

With the right theme and the appropriate décor one can throw a party without having to look for a particular reason.

A new broom sweeps clean:
House-warming party

Moving into a new home and starting a new life is always a good reason for having a party – particularly when moving into a home you have built yourself. Of course, you can wait to have the house-warming party when everything is perfect, when the new furniture is in its place, the carpets laid and the curtains hung. There is more "atmosphere", however, in having a party when things are still under construction, so to speak. Also, spilled red wine will not matter as much.

It is specially nice for the host if the guests have actually helped with all the work involved in moving house. The party is then a sort of reward, be it lunchtime drinks or an evening "do". Invite everyone who has helped you over the last couple of days, but also those who regrettably had no time to help you this time around. A house-warming party is also a good opportunity for making the first contact with your neighbors. Even if you are not going to invite them, it is a good idea to inform them in advance of your plans, as neighbors who were annoyed by the sounds of your moving in might turn out to be difficult partners in future too.

DÉCOR In fitting with the reason for the party, it is quite all right for a house-warming party to have an improvised air. Well-filled moving boxes and sturdy trestle tables make good seats and tables. Instead of the fine damask tablecloth still packed in some box or other, a sheet on the discard list will do as well. If there is time to make decorations, an arrangement including bread, salt and small coins is suitable for this occasion. These are symbols of luck when taking up residence in a new apartment or moving into a house you have built yourself, and are usually brought by the guests. Wrap the bread in clear paper, pour the salt into a little bag made of jute or other material, glue the pennies onto the bag and tie the bag in its turn to the bread with string or thread. The whole arrangement makes a decorative center piece for the buffet.

BUFFET On the trestle tables you can have a simple buffet with food such as ham and cheese, stew, sausages, rissoles, potato salad, fish salad and similar uncomplicated things. Hearty granary bread and rolls are a good accompaniment. The traditional drink for this occasion is bottled beer which can be served from the crates without any fuss. The empty – and well-washed – bottles make good candlesticks for a house-warming party. Of course it is un-

derstood that you will also have a selection of nonalcoholic drinks available. Depending on the number of people at your party, you can use either the bathtub or a bucket filled with ice as a wine-cooler.

THEME PARTY A house-warming party can be turned into a humorous theme party without any trouble. The theme here is obvious – workmen. Your party will have a special atmosphere in which everything works together, the perhaps not-quite-finished apartment itself, the unpacked boxes everywhere, the walls still smelling of fresh paint and so on and so forth. With the right music, delicious food and – this is the guests' department – good humor, the mood of your party will take care of itself.

When sending the invitations, ask your friends to come to your party dressed as workmen. The necessary "costume" can surely be found in any household. An old pair of jeans, the older the better in

HINT Plastic cups, plates and cutlery are of course an easy solution, but problematic from an ecological point of view. At least for the crockery there is a sensible alternative which has been around for a few years: edible plates and bowls made of a waffle-like material that can either be eaten as a sort of bread or thrown away with no qualms with the other leftovers.

this case; down-at-heel trainers (sneakers); a faded T-shirt; an old cap or a painter's hat made of folded newspaper. The costume can be rounded off professionally with articles from various trades: an old paintbrush, a hammer or even just a screwdriver will do the trick.

Menu

Whisky sour

Stuffed pita bread

Cream of tomato soup

Garlic potatoes

Marinated carrots with sweet basil

Cold roast pork

Apple and vanilla ice-cream

Whisky sour

Preparation time: 5 minutes

For one glass:

45 ml/1½ fl oz (3 tablespoons) Scotch whisky

30 ml/1 fl oz (2 tablespoons) lemon juice

15 ml/½ fl oz (1 tablespoon) syrup

ice cubes

lemon peel to garnish

❶ Pour the Scotch whisky, lemon juice, syrup and ice cubes into a cocktail shaker and shake well. Pour through a sieve (strainer) into a cocktail glass. Garnish with lemon peel.

Stuffed pita bread

Preparation time: 40 minutes

2 large pita breads

300 g (2 medium) red bell peppers

300 g (2 medium) yellow bell peppers

400 g (2 large) green bell peppers

10 tablespoons olive oil

herb salt

freshly ground pepper

3 cloves of garlic

500 g/1 lb mozzarella cheese

❶ Cut the pita breads in half lengthways, hollow out carefully, leaving an edge on one side free.

❷ Cut the bell peppers into quarters, remove seeds, wash and dice finely. Heat 6 tablespoons of olive oil in a pan, add the peppers and sauté, season with herb salt and pepper and cook gently. The peppers should still be crisp.

❸ Peel the garlic and finely chop. Drain the mozzarella and dice. Mix the garlic and mozzarella with the rest of the oil and add herb salt to taste.

❹ Spread the pepper mixture onto the bottom half of the pita bread, arrange the mozzarella over it. Cover with the top half of the bread.

❺ Bake the pitas in a pre-heated oven at 200°C, 400°F, gas mark 6 for ten minutes until the cheese has melted.

Cream of tomato soup

Preparation time: 60 minutes

❶ Mash the tomatoes with a fork. Peel and chop the onions. Set half the chopped onions aside and cover. Wash, peel and chop the vegetables. Dice the bacon.

❷ Heat the olive oil in a large pan and fry the bacon. Add the onions and vegetables and let everything steam for about 5 minutes. Add tomatoes and the meat broth. Wash and dry the parsley, pluck the leaves from the stems and add to the soup. Cover the pot and simmer for about 15 minutes then pass through a sieve (strainer).

❸ Peel the garlic. Heat the butter in a second pan and sauté the rest of the onions until they become transparent. Add the garlic and sauté briefly with the onions. Sift the flour, sprinkle over the onions and cook for about 3 minutes stirring constantly. Pour the tomato sauce over the mixture, bring to the boil, lower heat and simmer for 10 minutes. Add salt, pepper and sugar to taste.

❹ Whip the cream until it is almost firm. Pour the soup into soup plates and decorate with a dab of whipped cream.

1 kg/2 lb 3 oz tinned (canned) tomatoes

150 g onions

2 bunches of vegetables for the soup broth (leeks, carrots, celery etc.)

150 g/5 oz slice streaky bacon

4 tablespoons olive oil

1½ liters instant meat broth

2 bunches of parsley

3 cloves of garlic

80 g/2¾ oz (⅓ cup) butter

60 g/2 oz (½ cup) plain (all-purpose) flour

salt

freshly ground white pepper

sugar

250 ml/8½ fl oz (1 cup) single (whipping) cream

Garlic potatoes

Preparation time: 1 hour and 10 minutes

❶ Peel the potatoes and cut into thin slices. Pat dry with kitchen paper. Peel the cloves of garlic and crush with a garlic press. Grease two shallow baking dishes. Spread crushed garlic onto the base of dishes. Pre-heat the oven to 200°C, 400°F, gas mark 6.

❷ Arrange a quarter of the potatoes into each dish, add salt and pepper. Sprinkle the cheese over the potatoes and dot flakes of butter. Cover with the remaining potatoes and repeat. Pour cream along the edge of each dish. Bake in the oven for 30 to 40 minutes until golden-brown.

2 kg/4½ potatoes

4 cloves of garlic

fat or oil for the baking dish

salt

freshly ground pepper

100 g/3½ oz grated Emmental or Gouda cheese

120 g/4¼ oz (½ cup) butter

600 ml/20 oz (2½ cups) single (whipping) cream

A small celebration with colleagues:
The office party

Nothing should stand in the way of having a party at work for either of the following reasons: celebrating starting a new job and having a leaving party. There are of course a myriad of other reasons for having parties at work. Depending on the atmosphere and mood of the work place one can celebrate birthdays, motherhood, fatherhood, promotion, the clinching of a good deal, having worked for the firm for many years or even just the 1000th hour of overtime this year!

If the food is being brought to the work place, then it is obviously those foods that can be made in advance and that keep well are most suitable. In a large firm it might be worth speaking to the management of the canteen about catering for a party in your department. You can also find out if you will be able to borrow dishes, glasses and cutlery for the celebration. Most canteens are prepared for such requests and have a list of prices for the renting and cleaning of plates, glasses etc. Most office workers already have little snacks hidden in their desks, but it is of course nicer to prepare a proper buffet when throwing a party. Depending on the degree of camaraderie amongst colleagues, one can ask for their help with the preparations.

BUFFET If the celebration is taking place in an office, then the desks and other furniture will be suitable for setting out the buffet. Paper tablecloths or ones made of waxcloth and a large bunch of flowers will easily turn the sober workaday atmosphere into a pleasant place to have a party. Sometimes it is possible to include the hallway in the party area. This is a good idea when the rooms are cramped

and the department is spread over a number of offices.

DÉCOR The décor need not be too lavish, as otherwise work will be disturbed for too long when putting up and taking down the decorations. This is also true when the party is taking place in the company canteen as this is used by all members of a firm. As a party at work usually only lasts a couple of hours anyway, the decorations can have a slightly improvised air. If the lighting is all too bright and glaring, it can be softened with candlelight.

Whether or not the party is being organized by an individual or by several people, there are a couple of points that need to be clear before things get off the ground:
• is having a party at one's place of work even allowed?
• on which level is the decision made?
• is it possible to give the party a theme?
• will it be possible to decorate the invitations in an original way in line with the theme?
• which colleagues are to be invited?

- are family members and other guests from outside the firm to be invited?
- which day of the week and what time will be least likely to disturb the general running of the firm?
- on which day can most of the people being invited attend?

If parties on the firm premises are forbidden by the management, there are always alternative venues. How about a boat trip or a country walk? Office parties do not always have to be held during work hours. If you decide on a trip to the country, it might be a good idea to start planning a couple of weeks in advance. Undertaking communal activities

HINT Alcoholic beverages should not play a major role when planning an office party. It is better to offer mineral water, juices, coffee and tea. Many firms forbid the drinking of alcohol on the premises anyway. Therefore, whoever is applying for permission for the party should perhaps ask about an exception for alcoholic drinks and tobacco.

with colleagues is always beneficial for the atmosphere at work.

Menu

Alcohol-free ginger apple cocktail

Tuna dip with vegetables

Meatballs

Smoked pork loin

Pasta salad with feta cheese

Cappuccino cream

Alcohol-free ginger apple cocktail

Preparation time: 3 minutes

1 liter/33 fl oz (4 cups) apple juice

½ liter/17 fl oz (2 cups) ginger ale

juice of 3 to 4 limes

½ liter/17 fl oz (2 cups) mineral water

ice cubes

apple wedges to garnish

juice of 1 lemon

❶ Mix the apple juice and ginger ale in a large jug. Press the limes and add the juice to the apple juice. Fill up with mineral water.

❷ Put two ice cubes in each glass and fill with the cocktail. Sprinkle lemon juice over the apple wedges and use them to decorate the rims of the glasses.

HINT Moisten the rims of the glasses and dip into sugar. This is a very decorative touch.

Tuna dip with vegetables

Preparation time: 45 minutes, plus the time it takes to cool

550 g/20 oz tinned (canned) tuna in oil

250 g/8¾ oz (1 cup) crème fraîche

350 g/12 oz cream cheese

1 large bunch chives

1 bunch dill

juice of 2 or 3 lemons

½ teaspoon sugar

herb salt

2 tablespoons capers

❶ Drain the tuna in a sieve (strainer), break up with a fork. Mix with the crème fraîche in a blender or with a hand-held mixer until creamy. Stir in the cream cheese a spoonful at a time.

❷ Wash the chives and dill and pat dry. Snip the chives into little rolls. Strip the dill leaves from the stalks and chop finely. Press (squeeze) the lemons.

❸ Stir the herbs into the dip and add lemon juice, sugar, herb salt and pepper to taste. Spoon into a glass bowl and garnish with the capers.

HINT Suitable things to use for dipping are bread sticks and raw vegetables cut into sticks. Try asparagus, carrots, celery sticks and courgettes (zucchini) as well as chicory leaves and radishes. Wash the vegetables, cut into strips about 5cm (2 in) long. Halve the chicory and large radishes. Arrange nicely on a plate.

Meatballs

Preparation time: 30 minutes plus cooling time

❶ Soak the slices of toast in warm water, press the water out and mix with the minced meat. Peel the onions and garlic. Chop the onions finely and crush the garlic with a garlic press. Wash the parsley, pat dry and chop finely. Grate cheese finely.

❷ Add the onions, garlic, cheese, eggs, vinegar and olive oil to the meat mixture and mix well. Add salt, pepper and oregano, cover and set aside somewhere cool for 30 minutes.

❸ Scoop out spoonfuls of the mixture and form into balls. Roll in flour. Heat enough oil in a large frying pan and fry the meatballs in batches from all sides until golden brown. Drain on crumpled kitchen paper (paper towel).

4 slices of toast

1 kg/2 lbs 3 oz minced (ground) meat (pork or lamb)

3 onions

4 cloves of garlic

2 bunches of parsley

150 g/5¼ oz strong-flavored cheese

2 eggs

2 teaspoons vinegar

2 teaspoons olive oil

salt

freshly ground pepper

1 teaspoon chopped oregano

flour for dusting

oil for frying

Smoked pork loin

Preparation time: 1 hour and 30 minutes

2 kg/4½ lbs smoked pork loin

3 tablespoons horseradish

1 tablespoon lemon juice

freshly ground pepper

5 tablespoons oil

grease for the roasting dish

❶ Pre-heat oven to 200°C, 400°F, gas mark 6. Wash the pork loin and pat dry. Mix the horseradish with the lemon juice, some pepper and the oil. Spread the marinade evenly over the joint.

❷ Put the meat in a greased roasting tin and roast in the oven for about 1 hour basting regularly with the meat juices. Turn oven off and leave to rest for another 10 minutes. Remove from oven, cut into slices and allow to cool.

> **HINT** Serve a small bowl each of creamy horseradish sauce and medium strong mustard with the roast. Don't forget to put salt and pepper on the table.

Pasta salad with feta cheese

Preparation time: 35 minutes

250 g/½ lb pasta (macaroni, pasta shells etc.)

salt

200 g/7 oz feta cheese

250 g/9 oz cherry tomatoes

2 large yellow bell peppers

8 artichoke hearts (tinned)

100 g/3½ oz black olives

1 clove of garlic

85 ml/3 fl oz (⅓ cup) olive oil

4 to 5 tablespoons white wine vinegar

freshly ground pepper

2 bunches of sweet basil

❶ Cook the pasta in boiling, salted water according to the instructions on the packet. Drain through a sieve (strainer) and allow to cool.

❷ Cut the feta cheese into cubes. Wash the cherry tomatoes and cut in half. Wash and quarter the peppers, remove seeds and dice. Drain the artichoke hearts and cut into quarters. De-stone (pit) the olives and cut into strips. In a large bowl mix all the prepared ingredients with the pasta.

❸ Peel the garlic, crush in the garlic press and mix with the oil and vinegar. Add pepper to taste. Pour this marinade over the salad and mix everything carefully.

❹ Wash the sweet basil, pat dry and cut the leaves into strips. Sprinkle over the salad and mix in carefully. Leave the salad in a cool place overnight to marinade.

Cappuccino cream

Preparation time: 20 minutes, plus cooling time

❶ Heat the cappuccino (coffee) with the milk and vanilla sugar while stirring constantly. Do not allow to boil.

❷ Soak the gelatine in cold water. Beat the egg yolks with the powdered sugar until foamy. Gradually stir in the hot cappuccino a little at a time.

❸ Whip this mixture over a hot double boiler. Press out the gelatine, add to the pot and allow to dissolve. Now keep stirring the mixture but over a cold double boiler until it cools and starts to gel.

❹ Whip the cream and fold into the cooled mixture. Pour into two bowls, cover and set aside for two hours to cool.

❺ Decorate the dessert with the sifted cocoa and powdered sugar.

500 ml/17 fl oz (2 cups) strong cappuccino (coffee)

400 ml/14 fl oz (1⅔ cups) milk

3 sachets vanilla sugar

8 leaves white gelatin

8 egg yolks

140 g/5 oz (1⅛ cups) powdered sugar

500 ml/17 fl oz (2 cups) single (whipping) cream

cocoa powder and powdered (whipping) sugar to sprinkle over

HINT Serve sponge fingers or wafers with the cappuccino cream. You can also serve espresso if there is an espresso machine in your office.

Checklist

The day before the party
- [ ] make the tuna dip
- [ ] fry the meatballs
- [ ] make the pork loin roast
- [ ] make the pasta salad without adding the tomatoes or the sweet basil
- [ ] make the cappuccino cream
- [ ] prepare ice cubes

On the morning of the party
- [ ] mix the ginger apple cocktail and pour into bottles
- [ ] cut the apple wedges and sprinkle with the lemon juice
- [ ] prepare the vegetables for the tuna dip
- [ ] garnish the cappuccino cream
- [ ] buy fresh bread and slice

The big day for little people:
A children's party

Looking forward to something with anticipation is almost as much fun as the thing itself. This is particularly so for children in the weeks and days preceding their birthday. However, parents tend to look forward to the big day with mixed feelings as there will be a lot of work involved with feeding and entertaining a number of children from around the neighborhood and school. Lucky are they whose children were born in the summer and who own a big garden with a lawn. This is the ideal place for the small guests to run around and play.

Not every child who has ever invited your child to his or her birthday needs to be invited back in return, but children have a very delicate sense of what is important and what is not. Therefore, rather than causing the small host undue distress, why not invite two or three more guests than were originally planned for? In order to keep some sort of control over the celebration, invite another friendly mother along to the party to give you some support. A father will do just as well, of course.

The menu does not have to be too fancy or lavish for a children's party: fairly simple sweet cakes, chocolate pudding, large trays of pizza, rissoles, pasta salad, or chips with ketchup are the most favorite foods, and sweet lemonade and iced fruit tea are the preferred drinks.

As children love dressing up, we have two suggestion for theme parties with fancy dress.

Party theme "Ghost party"

The basic colors for the ghost birthday party could be black, white and a bilious green. These colors should be repeated in most of the decoration. It is particularly ghoulish if you have a room that can be darkened and the lights covered with green crepe paper. If the children are given torches (flashlights) they can make an eerie atmosphere.

INVITATION CARDS Write the following text on white paper and then roll it up and put it into a balloon that has not been blown up yet. Every guest has to blow up the balloon at home and burst it with a pin before he or she can read the invitation. "The Great Ghost, Headless Max, invites you to his creepy-fun birthday party in Castle Tremblestone. Please come at ...o'clock Earth-time in your ghostly costume and bring along a torch (flashlight)."

TABLE DECORATION Blow up a white balloon for each child. Paint on a ghostly face with a black waterproof pen (see sketch). Cut black crepe paper into 50 cm (20 in) long and 5 cm (2 in) wide strips and glue to the top of the balloon as hair. Tie a string to each balloon with a name card at the end and attach them to the chairs. Each child will be able to find his or her place at the birthday table straight away.

SPIDER'S WEB GAME
Materials:
Different colored balls of wool, cardboard name cards (4 x 8 cm) and small, wrapped presents, as many as there are children.

Preparation:
A length of wool about 8m (25 ft) long is cut for each guest. Tie the name card to one end and a present to the other. Then each string is wound through the room, around the chair legs, under the cupboards and so on.

The game:
Each child looks for his or her name card and has to unravel the length of wool in order to reach the present at the other end. This is a good game for the beginning of the party as the children get to know each other more quickly.

Children's cake with smarties

Preparation time: 1 hour and 20 minutes

❶ Pre-heat oven to 180°C, 350°F, gas mark 4. Melt the butter in double boiler while stirring constantly and allow to cool a little.

❷ Add the eggs to the melted butter and stir in well. Stir in the flour and sugar gradually.

❸ Grease a baking tin and sprinkle with flour. Spoon in cake mixture and bake for about 45 minutes. Test with a cake needle to see if done.

❹ Turn the cake out onto a rack to cool. Decorate with smarties (M&Ms) and birthday candles.

200 g/7 oz butter

4 eggs

200 g/7 oz plain (all-purpose) flour

200 g/7 oz sugar

grease and flour for the cake tin

1 packet smarties (M&Ms)

small birthday candles

Checklist

The day before the party
☐ prepare the meat patty centipede (steps 1–2)

☐ bake and decorate the children's cake

On the morning of the party
☐ make the apple juice punch and keep cool

☐ make the tomato toadstools

3 to 4 hours before the guests arrive
☐ make the hotdog pasta salad (do not put in refrigerator)

½ to 1 hour before the guests arrive
☐ finish making the meat patty centipede (step 3)

Creating individual invitations and decorations

Among the preparations for a party that are the most fun are the making of the invitations, name cards and the menus. There are no limits to your imagination but the appearance of the invitation as well as the other cards and documents should be in line with the kind of party being planned. If you are unsure about some aspect then you can find help in the relevant shops where you will also find the necessary materials: paper and card, paints and ink, pens and brushes. This is the time for those family members or friends who can draw to show what they can do.

Using the computer

If you cannot draw and have no-one to help you, then do not despair as we live in the age of the computer and documents pleasing to the eye can also be made by those of us who have little artistic talent. The machine is, of course, no substitute for good taste and a sense of style, but you will find what you think is suitable for you and your guests after some experimenting. Most computer software today contains drawing and painting programs that can be combined with the word processing. With these, and a little practice, it is easy to turn your various texts into small works of art with graphic or artistic elements. Often the computer has a myriad of symbols which can be used:
bubbling champagne glasses, clowns' faces, maps of the world, Christmas trees and many others. More and more households own scanners and digital methods of making pictures by which means photographs can also be incorporated into a design.

When looking at the cornucopia of typefaces, type size, photography motifs and graphic elements, it might be well to remember that for all creative – and other – occupations: less is sometimes more.

The materials are important

When choosing paper one should take care not to buy a quality that is less than 80mg per square metre. This is the normal weight for typing paper and printers of the usual type. It also means that you can put three sheets in an envelope without being over the 20 g limit of a standard letter. For invitations, congratulations and name cards, card between 150 and 200 g is suitable.

Any up-to-date copy shop will be able to reproduce your design with decent color quality. Printing them out singly at home can take a long time and, if you take the paper and toner into account, is not necessarily cheaper. If you are sending out invitations for a big wedding you should probably think of getting professional help anyway. A printer is the right person to consult if you need a really large quantity. Apart from the larger selection of paper, card and typefaces, you will get good, professional advice which you cannot get from your computer at home nor from your local copy shop.

On the following pages you will find several motifs as suggestions for decorating your party. Using a copier, these designs are easy to reproduce onto name cards for the table and invitations as well as for table decorations.

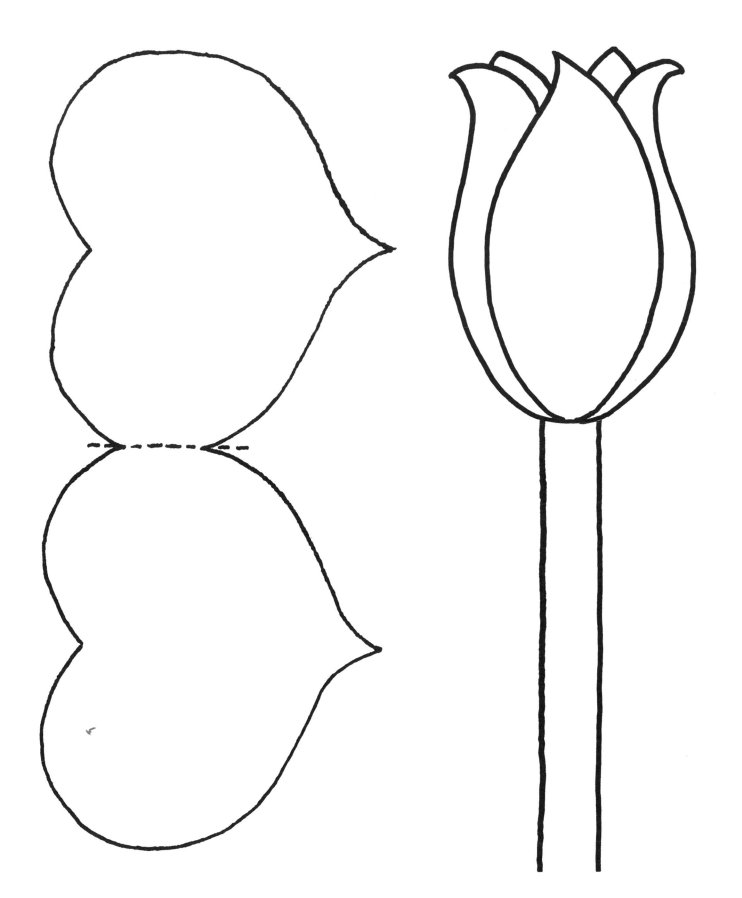

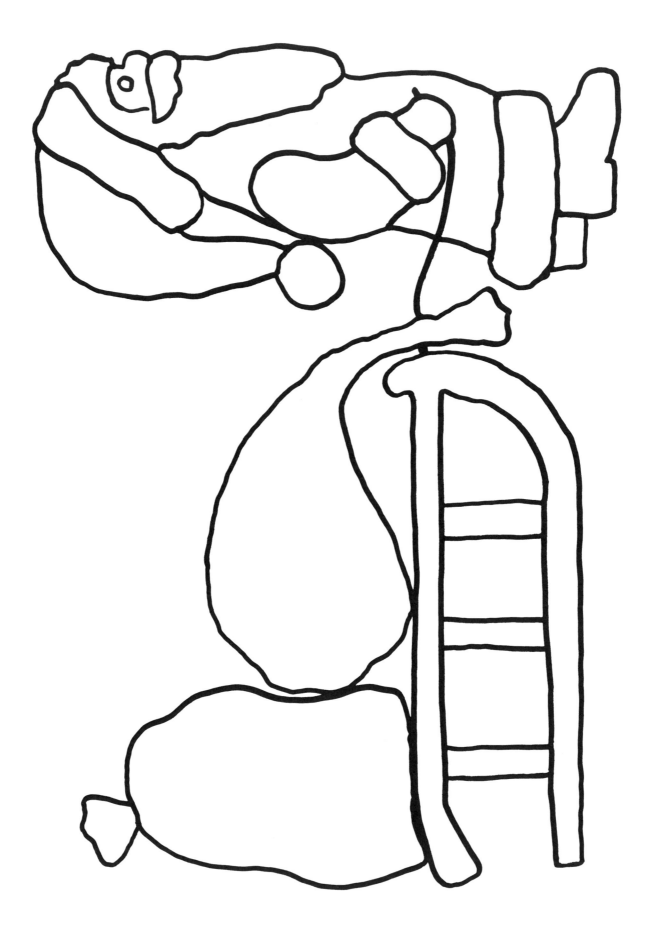

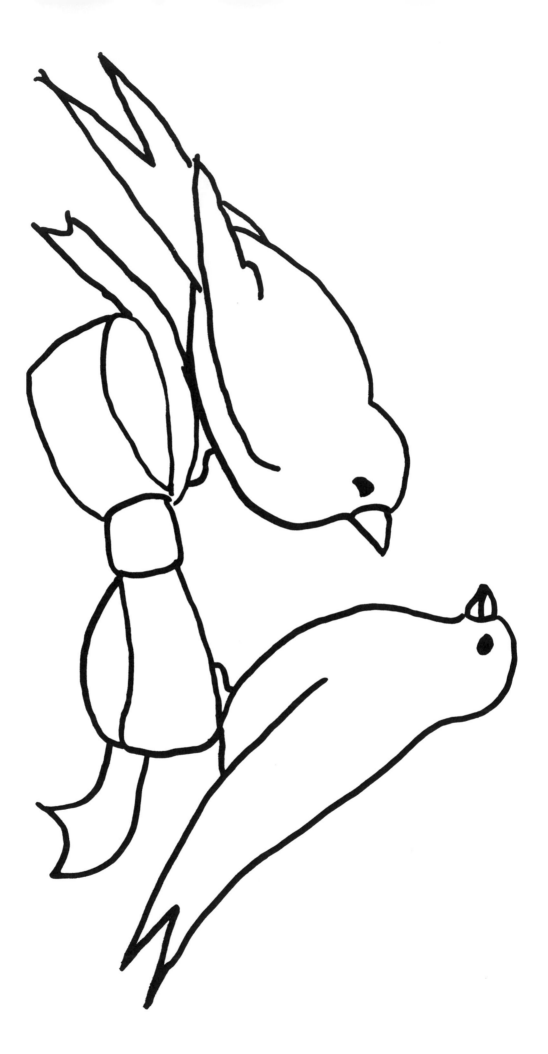

Index

Concept and execution:
Twin Books, Munich

Text: Andrea Wrobel, Dagmar Gronius-Gaier,
Mathias Hejny, Sabine Kurz, Christa Pöppelmann,
Michaela Didyk

Translation: (p. 1–47): Anthea Bell in association
with First Edition Translations Ltd., Cambridge, UK;
(p. 48–236): Greta Dunn in association with Twin
Books, Munich

Editing: Lin Thomas in association with First Edition
Translations Ltd., Cambridge, UK

Type setting: The Write Idea in association with
First Edition Translations Ltd., Cambridge, UK;
HUBERT Medien Design, Munich

Printing: Druckerei Appl, Wemding

© 2001 DuMont Buchverlag, Köln
(monte von DuMont)
All rights reserved

ISBN 3-7701-7042-3

Printed in Germany

Picture acknowledgments:
The editors and publishers thank the following for
their help in the creation of this book:

Grüne Erde: S. 14, 24
Alno: S. 15, 19, 34, 50, 194
Brigitte Sporrer: S. 6, 11, 13, 20, 23, 36, 37, 54, 55,
64, 65, 67, 68, 74, 77, 82, 86, 95, 96, 98, 106, 107,
109, 116, 119, 127, 135, 138, 144, 147, 156, 158,
160, 163, 176, 181, 182, 188, 192, 196, 198, 201,
207, 216